SOUL MATES

A New Age Guide to Finding Your One True Love

Terra Wolfe

Citadel Press
Kensington Publishing Corp.
www.kensingtonbooks.com

CITADEL PRESS books are published by

Kensington Publishing Corp.
850 Third Avenue
New York, NY 10022

All Kensington titles, imprints, and distributed lines are available at special quantity discounts for bulk purchases for sales promotions, premiums, fund raising, educational, or institutional use. Special book excerpts or customized printings can also be created to fit specific needs. For details, write or phone the office of the Kensington special sales manager: Kensington Publishing Corp., 850 Third Avenue, New York, NY 10022, attn: Special Sales Department, phone 1-800-221-2647.

First printing 2000

10 9 8 7 6 5 4 3 2 1

Printed in the United States of America

Library of Congress Cataloging-in-Publication Data
Wolfe, Terra.
    Soul mates : a new age guide to finding your one true love
/ Terra Wolfe.
      p. cm.
      ISBN 0-8065-2101-5 (pbk.)
    1. Soul mates. 2. Soul mates—Case studies. 3. Man-woman relationships—
Miscellanea. 4. Karma. I. Title.
BF1045.I58W65 1999
646.7'17—dc21   99-25915
                                                       CIP

Asleep, awake, by night or day
The friends I seek are seeking me.

No wind can drive my barque astray.
Nor change the tide of destiny.

The stars come nightly to the sky,
The tidal wave unto the sea.

Nor time, nor space, nor deep nor height
Can keep my own away from me.

—John Burroughs

To Alexandria,
who makes my life brighter.
May her life and loves
be easier than her Grandmama's,
but no less interesting.

CONTENTS

Beginning to Connect; Keeping It Working—The Beginning;
Beyond the Beginning—The Transition After the First
Month; A Little Bit About Sexuality; Other People—
Blending Family, Friends, and Work Relationships;
Restructuring—Changes That Keep It Going; Sometimes It's
Not Forever; Surviving a Breakup

Obsession Is Not Love; Healing; Moving On, Moving Up;
The Wisdom to Know the Difference—Beginning Again
With More Clarity

"DOES HE LOVE ME?"
ISN'T THE QUESTION

Love works a different way in different minds
The fool it enlightens and the wise it blinds.

—John Dryden

I hear the question every day: "Does he love me?" "Does she love me?"—as though the answer to this question will solve any problem and overcome any obstacle in a relationship. A better question is "How does he or she love me?"

A soul mate is *not* a person who comes into your life and loves you the way you want to be loved. Rather, a soul mate will often love you the way you *need* to be loved. The purpose of a soul mate is to assist in your growth.

If you would like to find a soul mate who honors you, you must begin to honor yourself. If you want a soul mate to understand you, you must try understand yourself. It is a law of the universe that you will receive what you give. If you would like to find unconditional love, learn to love unconditionally.

When we need to learn life lessons, Spirit has a way of helping us by sending soul mates who will appear at appropriate times in our lives according to the lessons that we need to learn. These soul mates are not people we learn to love; they are people we have already loved in past lifetimes. If we are open to them when they come into our lives, we will recognize them .

Granted, most people don't say, "There's my soul mate now." But there is a unique feeling, a difference, right away, with soul mates. They feel more "real" than other people; there is an intensity to them from the beginning. This is because when you are soul mates, *you have been together before*. There is the immediate recognition of a beloved soul.

———

Emily's good friend Shelly introduced her to Jake. Emily felt that there was something very intense about Jake right away. Through the evening it built. The next day they had lunch. By the weekend, they were planning to move in together. They just wanted to be together all the time. It was like meeting a brother, a lover, a best friend.

Jake was an attorney and had to consider the proprieties. It was important to him what other people thought. He also had some unfinished business with an old girlfriend. Things kept getting in the way. Still, they both tried to work it out. There was something compelling about the way the two of them felt when they were together.

Life, though, was throwing too many obstacles in the way for them to work it out. On the last night they were together, Jake said, "I feel really guilty about you because we were married once and I left you. I went off to the Crusades and was killed."

Emily was amazed, Jake had just described the only past life that she really remembered: She had remembered it since she was a little girl. In that life, she had been married at twelve and her husband had gone away almost immediately. She'd never heard from him again.

They shared stories about the life when they were married so briefly. Once they understood the experience, it was easier to release the relationship, which was obviously not meant to be.

Within a year she was happy in a life she could not have had if she had been unable to let go of this compelling man.

———

Jake and Emily's was a soul-mate relationship. It had no "happily ever after," but it served a purpose of assisting learning and growth. It was intense, compelling, and it released once the karmic transaction had been accomplished. In this case the transaction was love and forgiveness.

Not all relationships last forever. However, this doesn't mean it was a negative experience. Some of the most intense and growth-providing relationships are short term. Some, however, last far longer.

———

Beth was seventeen and Justin was fifteen. They met in high school. They looked alike even then. They recognized each other at once and began dating. Within the year they had found a way to sleep together every night without their parents' knowledge.

They both went to excellent colleges and stayed together. Right after college, they married.

They had two little blond children, grew to look even more like brother and sister, and lived in a lovely old Victorian house in the farthest suburbs more or less happily ever after.

———

This is the sort of soul-mate story we all want to hear. However, this sort of experience really can't happen unless the two of you meet when you are young and grow up together.

The older you get, the more complicated the relationship gets, because you are already psychologically formed. This doesn't mean that you don't have a soul mate or two out there; it only means you have to get a bit realistic about what kind of relationship is possible.

There are other reasons why Beth and Justin lived happily ever after. It could have been just the luck of the draw. Both of these kids were from families that were intelligent, articulate, wealthy. By the time they met, they both had extraordinary communication skills. They used these skills to determine their emerging value system together. They came from similar backgrounds, so their values were very similar, too. They discovered sex together, understood each other very well in that area.

But beyond those things, the karma evident in this sort of situation is amazing. Obviously Beth and Justin had every intention of being born into a life that would let them get together while they were young. They had without a doubt been together in many past lives as mates, and had completed some serious karmic work in past lives. This life was a reward for them and a learning process that could be taken slowly and carefully.

We all have our karma. Discovering our own karmic pattern is the first step to revealing what sort of soul mates we can expect. We will also learn what to do to keep them in our lives so we can continue to learn and grow from them.

Intentionally bringing a soul mate into your life requires understanding the karmic process. It also demands that you get on the path to your own growth, and it requires relationship skills.

If you are looking for someone to provide you with a sensible relationship, you are not looking for a soul mate. You are looking for a business partner. Soul-mate love can be crazy, fascinating, and compelling. It can take your breath away and can be everything your mother warned you against. You must be brave, because you must be willing to offer your soul mate your whole heart and not be afraid to lose it.

It is like dancing on a sword's edge. It is the joy of finding someone who sees you and loves you for yourself, not in spite of yourself. You feel as if you would sell a perfect marriage for twenty minutes with this person. You'd better be a romantic. Leave your cynical nature behind. This is the land of hopes and dreams. Enter at your own risk and for your own joy.

Can you make this love last a lifetime? Maybe; some do. But even if you don't, you can look your grandchild in the eye and say, yes, I have loved.

PART ONE

SOUL MATES IN YOUR LIFE

The Karma/Dharma Effect

I pray Thee for undying love. I pray Thee for the birthless state; but were I to be born again, for the grace of never forgetting Thee. Still more do I pray to be at Thy feet singing joyfully while You dance.

—Tirumurai 11, Karaikkal Ammaiyar

After death, the soul goes to the next world bearing in mind the subtle impressions of its deeds, and after reaping their harvest returns again to this world of action. Thus, he who had desires continues subject to rebirth.

—Shukla Yajur Veda, *Brihadaranyaka Upanishad* 4.4.6

It is impossible to understand the phenomenon of soul mate without knowing a little bit about karma. The word *karma* describes action that is the residue of past lives, and that is our assignment in this life. It is the action we come here to take. We fully participate in the decision to learn certain things and pay back certain debts accrued in past lives before we come into this one.

Karma is not about punishment or rewards, although these words may be used in describing it, because the concept is close.

If we begin to understand that all of our lives are learning experiences that allow us to grow into fully evolved souls, then periodically receiving rather difficult lives is not unlike taking an advanced placement course in school. To help us with our lessons, we are joined in each life by a family with whom we have worked

3

in different roles for many lifetimes. The decision to meet in this life is mutual and beneficial for each of us. These people are soul mates. They are not all lovers, of course.

Your best friend is probably a soul mate. Your family is always karmic family; you have been together before. Probably not the same way; your parents might have been your children, your brother in a past life might be a son in this one.

Families tend to reincarnate in groups. They might not necessarily be around in your early years, but some will be. Throughout your life they will appear, all in their own time. Don't worry about missing them. Miraculous things happen to draw them your way. Nothing can keep you from your karmic family when it is time for them to appear.

It is the time that each appears that is important. Your karmic soul mates come to help you work on your own growth. The issues you have decided to work on in this life are the issues that bring them into your life.

Two things, especially will be significant with a soul mate. The first is your own growth. The other is the soul growth of your partner. For instance, if you have lived a lot of past lives in which you were settled down with a family, you may choose to learn independence in this life. You will feel a real pull toward family, but life issues will keep you on your own. As you become more independent, you will find soul mates entering your life to support your growth in this direction. They will keep you in relationships that allow you to explore life more independently. This sort of interplay will be important for your partner's growth, too.

At certain ages, this issue will be different. In your twenties, for instance, when the tribal spirit is felt and you are seeking a safe place to have your children and nurture them, you may forget about independence altogether. But as you enter your thirties and want to become more yourself and less a member of a group, you will find a soul mate entering your life who will help you attain this independence.

Needless to say, it is not helpful to become dependent on this person. That is not the role for a soul mate in these circumstances. In its effort to bring you to your own independence, this relationship will not allow you to depend on it. This can be a hard lesson, but it puts you in the right energy for your life.

Once you begin to master and enjoy independence, you may find that a soul mate appears whose role is to join you in that independence; who will support and honor it.

This is one way that soul mates can interact. However, there are an infinite number of life dramas you can experience, but yours will be unique. What will be similar, though, is that at critical times soul mates will enter your life to help you on your path. Some are there for only a while; some come to stay forever.

The second significant soul-mate issue you may encounter is the payment of karmic debt. Some of us do only a little of this in a life; others come into a life to clean it all up at once.

Karmic debt accrues when you have made mistakes, perhaps hurt people or affected their growth in a negative way. This happens over lifetimes. You will find that when people to whom you owe a karmic debt come into your life, you will give them the help they need even if doing so takes you off your own path.

Sometimes you will find yourself in one relationship after another that seems to make no sense. You are doing a great deal for your partner and very little is coming your way from it, yet you keep on giving. Then suddenly it is over with little or no reason. If you have gotten past the illusion that things are supposed to be fair, you will be glad to see the end of it. The relationship no longer has any energy. The karma is now complete; move on.

Dharma is the service you provide to complete the karmic transaction. Dharma is selfless service, performed only for the goodness it brings. Usually this is a person-to-person transaction. In some cases, people come here to simply serve. Mother Teresa was a good example of a person who performed selfless service in places of desperate need.

Think of dharma as the sort of things we do for our children. They are a lot of work, but we really want our children to have that service. We want to take care of them. We have learned that part of the joy of having a baby is the experience of care-taking. That's when we see the first little smiles and the beginnings of their growth.

Often our karmic payback is this sort of service we do for another person. The people we pay back in this way... are they soul mates? You bet. This is not what you had in mind when you bought a book about soul mates. Still, you need to know this. And it gets better.

Soul mates have been members of our cosmic families since before our first incarnation. We have chosen to work together to complete our growth and learning in many arenas.

Your physical family is always karmic, as is anyone you have married or with whom you have had children. You can count on it.

Often when soul mates appear they seem like family, or remind you of someone in your family. Sometimes they just seem "more real" than anyone else in the room. Not every soul mate is a sexual connection, especially a karmic soul mate.

But since they travel in groups, you will often find that a soul mate brings a soul mate. If you are doing your work, that best friend of yours, whom you knew would be your best friend right away because she looks like your cousin, will often be the one to introduce you to the soul mate who knocks your socks off.

Soul mates are an invitation to growth. A soul mate will be your best teacher. This is not about happily ever after. The most effective way to end a soul-mate relationship is to limit your own growth. This life is an experience of growth and learning. Soul mates appear most often to those who are participating in that dance.

What Is a Soul Mate?

...whose any mystery makes every man's
flesh put space on; and his mind take off time.

—e. e. cummings

Let's start with the soul mates you don't really want to hear about and get them out of the way: mother, father, brothers, sisters, cousins, aunts, uncles, grandparents, sons, daughters, grandchildren, and usually those whom these people marry. You can add anyone you marry and anyone with whom you have children; in fact, add most of the people you have slept with.

Also include the people who have changed your life. A good example is the second-grade teacher who took the time to show you what you were good at. The driver of the car that nearly hit you and made you conscious of your life in a new way is also a soul mate. The friend who pulls you out of harm's way qualifies, too.

But the love we are all looking for is the partner who ignites our passion; the person who will perform with us the sacred ceremonies of love. You are seeking the one with whom you can join in the God-and-Goddess dance of the universe. Among this group of soul mates there are three distinct types.

The Karmic Connection

The first and most common is the karmic soul mate, who has been part of your karmic family since time began. You have birthed this one and held his head in your lap when he died. He has been your brother, your son, your teacher, and your enemy. All of these roles he performed with love and with the knowledge that he was providing you with the situation you need for growth and learning. You have done the same for him. In this life you might owe karmic debts to each other in many combinations. Or you might have planned to get together for just a while or for a life, because you know each other so well and enjoy being together.

This soul mate will usually feel very familiar and comfortable from the first time you see each other. In some cases there will be residue from less positive past lives, as in the case of Katherine and Guillermo.

Katherine walked into a meeting of her ski club. There were many friends and shared experiences in the several groups that met here and planned trips for the ski season. In one, a group of teachers who were old friends, she saw someone new and felt cold at once. The message she heard clearly was, "Oh no, it's him. He killed me."

She found reasons that night to stay far away from that group. For the next year, he was nearly always with them and she kept her distance. She did like these people, however, and would make it a point to talk to them when he was not around.

One night, when she was talking to one of the teachers, he walked right over to them before she could duck away. She was trying to back away when one of her friends introduced them.

"Katherine," he said, "this is Guillermo. He has been working with us for about six months." As her social instincts took over, she noticed that Guillermo had amazing eyes. He was very dark, but his eyes were bright blue. She was drawn to the sadness she saw in them.

Over the next few months she got to know him. Clearly there were things he wouldn't talk about. He often said that he was a very bad person. He told her that if she ever really got to know him, she would be appalled.

Katherine knew enough to stay away from a man who said things like this, but he seemed so troubled. She knew that a lot of what he was feeling came from a past life—and in that past life he had killed her.

She kept waiting for an opportunity to tell him. He kept avoiding any conversation that would allow her to get into the subject while still making his guilt clear to her.

Finally one night, when she felt that his need for comfort was so compelling she brought him home and made love to him.

As soon as she let herself feel love toward him, she felt released. The bond was broken. She realized that all she had to do was to love him. Once she understood that, she began to forgive him. Once that was done she was free of him. He was no longer compelling.

They remained friends. He still felt guilty. She was fond of him but no longer drawn to him. She offered one more time to tell him things that would help him heal. He could not accept that.

Soon he found a job in another city. She never saw him again.

———

It can be like that. The karmic exchange Katherine needed here was simply love. She needed to love and forgive her old enemy. For Guillermo, it was too difficult (as it often is for those who have been victimizers in another life) for him to let go of his guilt. Part of him wanted to do this, but he had held on to it for so long that he couldn't just let go. Hopefully, if he lets some love in, he will find it easier somewhere along the way. But Katherine had given him what she needed to give and for her, the karma was completed for this life. The energy of the relationship fell away.

Think of how much better it is this way than if she had allowed her feelings at the beginning to compel her to commit to this relationship. In her presence, Guillermo would always feel guilty and bad. Soon he would begin to resent her for loving him. Her love alone couldn't save him if he wasn't ready to save himself. It is the setup for a very painful time. Wisely, Katherine let the relationship go when she felt the energy release.

At the same time, it was a good thing to have shared this exchange. Katherine lost some of the fears that had been with her from this past-life experience. She began to see how love alone

could heal. Guillermo on some level knew that his victim had forgiven him. Eventually, that will help him release his guilt of being
a victimizer.

Relationships don't need to last a lifetime to have value.
Sometimes it is this very quality of transcience that allows a relationship to be intense enough to really push you into another way
of thinking. When a relationship is clearly not going to develop into
a life partnership then many things that might be significant in
another partner become irrelevant.

For instance, if you were looking for a mate, you might not
want to be involved with someone from an entirely different culture, because it could present many difficulties. Yet learning this
other culture intimately and lovingly could be a wonderful experience with a soul mate who is just going to be in your life, even for
a little while.

Try not to let yourself be shattered when these things end. You
will miss your soul mate, but release the experience lovingly.
Know that the growth this experience brought you will lead to
your ability to have better, more full relationships in the future.

The Karmic Life-Mate

we are for each other: then
laugh leaning back in my arms
for life's not a paragraph
And death i think is no parenthesis.

—e. e. cummings

The karmic mate is the one you already miss. You have been
together as partners so many times before. Occasionally you were
brother and sister or mother and son, but mostly you were partners. You raised children together, had successes and failures, tri-

umphs and tragedies. You held each other for the last breath and mourned the passing. You have been mates over the ages, often changing genders as you learned and grew over lifetimes.

We have not all done this in the same way. Many of us have had better than half of our past lives with the same partner—some even more. Some have been partners with two or three different souls over and over.

When you are having a hard day and wish for someone on whom to depend, you find yourself vaguely missing... someone. It is a person upon whom you have depended many times, and whom you almost always remember.

Needless to say, when you meet this person, you are pretty sure you have met someone very important to you. It may or may not be love at first sight, but you can be sure it will be memorable. When this person comes into your life, there will be an involvement. Often that involvement will end in marriage, especially if you meet early on in life.

———

In a lifetime Rachel recalled in a past-life regression while in her twenties, she remembered being married to a man whom she knew in this life to be Joel. That life was in northern Europe in the 1600s.

In this life, she had met Joel when she was eighteen, and they had married at twenty. They had three children and were very happy together and with their little family. She knew him to be her karmic mate and expected it to last for her whole life, as it had many times before.

But there was another part of the memory. In that old life, a brief flirtation with another man when she was thirty-five went nowhere because she was married. She had been very attracted to the man and had some romantic fantasies but it was unthinkable at that time to even entertain any further thought of him. Besides, she was thirty-five—too old to think herself attractive in an age when marriageable women were not over sixteen.

When Rachel was in her early thirties, she found her marriage to Joel falling apart. She couldn't understand why this was happening. He was her karmic mate. But nothing they did could save the marriage. She was still sad and confused when, at thirty-five, into her life walked a new man who brought her into quite a different relationship than the one she had known with Joel.

This man was romantic. He brought her flowers and courted her. She found herself flirting with him and giving in to her own romantic notions.

After a year or so, they were married. The marriage was not as easy and effortless as her first, but it was always interesting and she loved this man more than she ever could have imagined possible.

Guess who she found? The man she was so attracted to in her past life. She had completed her family work and decided to take a chance in this life and follow her heart. When her marriage fell apart and she was upset and confused, it was in order to make space for this love from the past whom she had never had a chance to be with before. Karma works its magic in many ways.

Beth and Justin, in the introduction to this book, were karmic mates, too. Often when we are thinking of a soul mate, it is this karmic mate we are seeking.

The karmic mate often appears when we are ready to settle down and have a family. Family is the theme of this kind of relationship. Such mates have also been known to appear later in life, after the adventures are done and the karmic payback has been accomplished, when we would like to join with our oldest love and just be happy for the rest of our life.

As you are beginning to see, karma can bring these people into our lives at any time, according to our own needs and plans.

The Twin Flame

At one glance I loved you with a thousand hearts.

—Mihri Hatun

The ultimate soul mate may or may not be any kind of a romantic encounter. In fact, you probably won't meet this person in your life; these relationships are very rare.

Sometimes twin flames will come together to accomplish something important in the world. Sometimes a twin flame will show up to give you exactly what you need to move to a higher level. I speak of higher levels here in the spiritual sense. There often is superconsciousness in a twin-flame relationship. Everything is more real; connections from this life or others seem obvious. There is a purpose to this relationship.

Everyone has a twin flame. The twin flame is another aspect of yourself. You have been traveling roads together from the beginning of time. Often your twin flame will not choose to reincarnate in the same time that you do; he or she will remain on the other side to assist you with your growth.

Often when you are on the planet together, you will choose to experience two totally different life paths. This way each of you can learn and grow and share that growth, for you are really a part of each other.

Twin flames may or may not even be of the opposite gender, although often they are, since the choice of each different experience adds to both souls' knowledge.

Wanting to find your own twin flame means that you long for a larger aspect of yourself. Your twin flame is always connected to you in an area that joins us that is beyond words. A pure flow of universal love contains your twin flame's communication with you.

Should you meet your twin flame in this world, prepare yourself: You have work to do. When twin flames choose to meet and work together, it is in order to change the world in a specific way. They use their lifetimes of knowledge to effect changes in the world that will lead to changes in consciousness in a very real way.

Twin flames might be working with many others to make these changes. But they have specific accomplishments that they are meant to bring into being.

Once you have met your twin flame, you are not looking at a comfortable domestic life, but a much larger agenda.

Your Own True Love

Love is the great miracle cure. Loving ourselves works miracles in our lives.

—Louise L. Hay

So with all the mates, karmic connections, and flames to deal with, who is your true love anyway? Who, after all, is the one person with whom you were meant to love and find joy and live your whole life? Who is the one person the universe supports in love and growth?

It is the one person those soul mates are here to love and teach and move toward the highest and best life. It is, of course, you.

You need to learn to love yourself, to honor yourself, to provide yourself with the nurturing you need, and to expect the very best in your life. That is the one sure thing that will begin to draw in the highest and best partner.

The soul mates who teach us the most difficult lessons appear when we do not honor ourselves. They come to teach us what happens in a relationship when we do not respect our own needs. These are the relationships we perceive as unfair—but this unfairness is really a tool to show you that you need to honor yourself. The partners who seemed like such jerks were jerks to teach you not to be one.

To stop living this kind of experience, you need to become the kind of spirit to whom your highest partner would be drawn.

The beginning of this process is to learn that you are Spirit's unique and wonderful creation. You need to celebrate that creature who yearns to grow and be seen for the exact, beautiful being that you are.

If you have ever loved someone who didn't love himself, you have experienced how impossible a thing it is to do. Such people suspect your love for them is something else. You must want something from them. Perhaps you want them to do something they don't want to do. They will believe anything but that you love them, because they can't comprehend it. They don't feel worthy of that love. They don't feel lovable.

If you don't feel lovable, if you don't know that you are presenting to the beloved the precious gift of your own love, then you will not draw to yourself the kind of person who can love you the way you want to be loved.

You will keep drawing the soul mates who will try to teach you what it is like when you don't love yourself, and you don't want any more of those relationships.

One way to begin to love yourself is to give yourself permission to be uniquely you. There is no need to transform yourself into someone else to be loved. In fact, that is the surest way not to be loved...what, then, would the other be loving?

When you are yourself at the right time and the right place in your growth you will be a magnet to the soul mate, who will love you as you are. There is no way to get to that without honoring yourself.

If you have repeatedly changed yourself to be what you thought someone else needed you to be, then you need to take some time off from the mating process and find yourself. Regather what you have let go in your efforts to please others. Think your own thoughts...take the time to find out what they are. Remember who you were when you liked yourself best. Be that.

You may have to go back to your childhood to find the beginnings of that person. You don't have to become a child; just try to remember who that child thought she was going to grow up to be.

There were things you believed in that you have no doubt put away because other people didn't like them. See if you want to take them back. There are things you never liked that you have done anyway because you thought they were expected. Stop doing these things. You may find that many of these things don't fit into your life now. But at least you'll see them and decide for yourself.

There is no blueprint for who you need to become, as long as it is you.

Another important issue in finally loving yourself is to begin forgiving. You need to forgive everyone who may have kept you from being yourself. And you need to forgive yourself.

You do not need to tell the others that you have forgiven them. Indeed, this is not usually a good idea; it makes them defensive and begins the process all over again. Just forgive them in your heart and release the energy. This is the most freeing thing you can do for yourself. You are not doing it for them. You are doing it so that you can stop carrying around so much unhappiness. Do yourself the favor of forgiving them all.

As you begin to forgive, a wonderful creature will begin to emerge. This is the self you want to be. Just enjoy being this person for a while. You have created this blessed soul; now you can begin to love it. Enjoy these moments of being alone with your newly acknowledged self.

Take some time to enjoy this, because a soul mate will come along soon, and you will be busy with partnership.

PART TWO

GETTING INTO THE RIGHT DANCE

If we are a metaphor of the universe, the human couple is the metaphor par excellence, the point of intersection of all forces and the seed of all forms. The couple is time recaptured, the return to the time before time.

—Octavio Paz

There is a natural learning process in life. Different ages require different lessons. A teenager who is trying to have the same kind of relationship as a thirty-year-old will face too many obstacles that his experience has not yet taught him to deal with.

Less obvious is the forty-year-old trying to conduct a relationship by the rules she learned as a teen.

For most of history, mating has been primarily reserved for teenagers. All of the structures as to what is appropriate or not have come to us from that time in our lives. In the past thirty years we have been trying to make new patterns as people have stayed unmarried longer and changed partners more often.

There have evolved certain patterns for each decade of growth. If you want to find the best soul mate, you need to be in a growth structure that is appropriate for your life.

It's an Age-Group Thing—How Relationships Change as We Grow

Gather ye rosebuds while ye may,
Old Time is still a-flying:
And this same flower that smiles today,
Tomorrow will be dying.
—Robert Herrick,
To the Virgins to Make Much of Time

The different kinds of relationships we need change as we grow. In each period of our growth, soul mates may appear to assist in our learning. We must remember that we are their soul mates, too. We teach as we learn.

If you stay in the right growth structure, you will meet the right soul mate. If, for instance, you are loving and relating by teenagers' rules when you are in your forties, you will not attract soul mates appropriate to your age. You will attract overage teenagers. They too will be off their own growth track, and will be disappointing partners.

The stages I will describe in the pages that follow are current socially. My years of counseling have taught me that the ages I indicate are when most people reach the given stages. There are exceptions to every rule, though; one big exception comes if child-bearing is delayed until the thirties and forties.

Children do well in a tribe; it gives them a structure and family group that is close and socializes them in a natural way. However, parents in their thirties and forties have quite outgrown the tribal model.

The forms that relationships take have shifted dramatically in the past hundred years. Less than a hundred years ago, most women had their babies beginning in their teens, when their bodies were most fertile. They had an extended family to help raise the children, and more children were welcomed.

Marriages happened earlier and most often lasted for the lifetime of the couple. Unfortunately, this lifetime was not that long. For most of the time when marriage meant "till death do us part," death occurred at around age thirty-five for at least one spouse.

Childbirth took many women, who were often pregnant every year throughout childbearing years. Epidemics, wars, and the sheer abuse of the body from decades of hard physical labor accounted for more. If you lived in a city your life span was shorter still, due to the appalling lack of sanitation there.

It is only the generations that came of age between the turn of the century until the early 1960s that married till death—and then found out how very long this was. By the 1970s, if a relationship didn't work the partners divorced—often to keep them from reliving what they saw as the awful example of their parents' unhappy marriage.

So socially, things have changed utterly in the last thirty years. There are lots of single people at every age. So, the old rules no longer apply, nor the old patterns of growth. We expect a lot more from our lives and our relationships than our mothers and grandmothers ever dreamed.

The speed of communication contributes to this new world. My grandmother assumed that most people worked in a factory or on a farm. She had no idea of the Lost Generation in Paris or the speakeasies in New York. She didn't know that women were throwing themselves on their husbands' pyres in India, or that there were still matrilineal cultures in the Pacific. Her life was traditional for her place and time. At fifteen she was young; at fifty she was old.

Contrast that to the life of her granddaughter. At fifty, I have traveled to Europe and to Mexico and the Caribbean. I have a reasonable expectation of seeing more of the world in the next twenty years. I have lived independently, raised a son alone after my divorce. I make my living with my head, not my hands.

I correspond with friends from Turkey to New Zealand. I am

very spiritual in ways that have nothing to do with my Baptist family roots. I have moved from the hills of a quiet village in upstate New York to the desert in Arizona. I live with two wolves, by choice. This is a world that my parents (who were, in their time, quite sophisticated) hardly understand. To my grand-mother it would be beyond comprehension.

I can't even imagine what sort of world my granddaughter will inhabit. It seems we are moving into a new age in many different ways. It is happening very fast.

Along with the changes in technology have come changes in behavior and even morality. The old rules no longer apply—and we have not yet found new ones to replace them.

So as I try now to explain the growth structure that our time seems to require, some parts will sound familiar and some will be new. Some will change soon. Some will take a decade. But one thing is for sure: This will not be the same world for long.

There are, of course, basic human issues that have remained the same since the days when we all lived in tribes. Try as we might to change them, they are part of our biology. We need to adapt to them.

Humans need a community of friends and relatives. We are tribal animals. We need food, structure, and shelter. We have a drive to procreate and nurture and protect our children. We have, at least, a habit of partnership with the opposite sex.

Such partnerships have varied widely through the ages. Most recently, they have taken the form of the marriage we are used to seeing in the West: one husband, one wife, till death do them part.

Although a significant number of people are still married in this way, a newer form of relationship known as serial monogamy is even more common. This relationship is monogamous for its dura-tion. Marriage may or may not be involved and when it is over, by consent (which is not always mutual), both partners seek new mates and form new monogamous relationships.

Yet many of us are trying to hold on to the old lifetime model of what a relationship should be.

What led to so drastic a change in our most personal relationships? There were may elements, some of which are contained in the technical advances we have taken for granted. These advantages brought with them enormous new knowledge and a potential for growth that was considered impossible when I was a child. New freedom and opportunities for growth mixing with our need for a tribe has meant the emergence of a new social paradigm.

This is reflected in our relationships. The person who was the moon and stars to you at eighteen doesn't look the same at thirty. Sometimes couples choose to make adjustments and work things through them. But these days people often choose to seek out a partner who suits the person they have become rather than the person they were.

Karmically, during this one life we may experience more than we did in nine or ten previous incarnations. Is it any wonder that we should be trying to even out more karma, or see ten or twelve soul mates appear, in such an age? In many ways, you might think of each stage I will describe below as the equivalent of a single life in other times.

This is not to say that you will have one soul mate for each ten years of your life. Many will find a karmic mate and stay with him or her for decades, working things out together. Still others will stay with a good partner for two or three decades and then choose not to have any more partners. Everyone does this in the way that suits them. No ways are right or wrong.

If you read this and are concerned that you have not proceeded through the stages in the manner I describe, relax. If you are paying attention, all of these things will happen. But you might miss one or the other passage at the time that is indicated. If this is the case, you will probably have this passage in a different way at a later time. Everyone passes through these stages at their own pace.

Seldom, however, will you experience these passages earlier than I discuss. You may have similar experiences, but these passages require a certain number of years under the belt in order to navigate properly.

First Love, Early Teens

The magic of first love is our ignorance that it can never end.

—Benjamin Disraeli

First love is often overwhelming. It happens when we have little or no experience with the intensity of a sexual connection. And because the hormones are surging in the teenage years, this relationship connects a couple on levels that seem to be the center of life itself. Since this relationship sets the tone for every subsequent romance, our expectations as to the joys or pains a sexual relationship will bring have their beginnings here.

Because expectations and beliefs that begin here are so powerful in future relationships, first love is tremendously important. Yet it happens at a time in life when although there are clearly the beginnings of adult physiology, those involved are hardly more than children.

It is a time when new feelings are everywhere and adolescent mood swings are in full gear. There is a tremendous restlessness in the air. And the teenagers involved:

- Don't know what they're doing
- Think everybody else knows what they are doing
- Act like they know what they are doing
- Will tell everybody that they know exactly what they are doing
- Claim that nobody understands them

If they were more experienced, maybe they wouldn't give love away so fully. And if they didn't do that, maybe they would never learn how amazing it can be to just let love become the whole reason for getting up in the morning. Of course the passion is intensified because there is always a bit of the forbidden about young love.

It is so important that this experience be honored. This is where future relationships begin to find their shape.

In the past, this first relationship was often the only relationship in a person's life. Indeed, humans seem to be set up for this intense mating experience very early. This is probably a biological imperative that was a very effective way to populate earth. The teen years have been a normal age for marriage or at least for mating through most of human existence, because the body of a teenage girl is the ideal place to make a baby. While this is a problem now, it has been very useful for humans in the past.

Children are still having children. It is biologically perfect. The female body in the teen years is very fertile and ready for childbearing. In *this* world, however, it is, socially, a train wreck.

In this complicated world, everybody needs an education into their twenties. What's more, we've moved away from living as extended families. Parents think their work is done with their own children and don't think their responsibility extends to their children's children. Which leaves the kids on their own as parents, and this really doesn't work.

We may eventually find that we cannot fight our biology, in which case we might just have to come up with a better way to take care of the kids. But for now it is a good idea not to have children in the first relationship.

The problem is that while the teenagers are having this relationship, they are sure that it's forever and the only love they will ever have. Women feel the first stirrings of yearning for a child. Young men want a permanent sexual partner. They only want to be together. And of course, they cannot be convinced that anyone understands how they feel.

Every day seems to hang on the interaction with the beloved, and every nuance of the relationship is examined. In a way, it is a shame kids can't just take a year off from school to deal with this. At this age, however, they need the structure of their peer group. That part of the tribe generally meets at school.

If you are in this stage, know that your first love is a very special kind of soul mate. You are teachers for each other. You have the sweet task of opening up new feelings, sexual emotions, for each other.

Since you have no real knowledge of such feelings yet, it is best to rely on your intuitions. I am not going to give any sexual education here. That depends on the cultural beliefs your family and friends have given you. But I will say a few things about what you might do to make this relationship the best it can be.

- Honor your feelings and the feelings of your beloved. Don't test them. These feelings are sacred gifts; treat them accordingly.

- Keep promises, secrets, and vows. Don't make them if you can't keep them.

- Don't have sex with someone who cannot talk about it with you. If you are not intimate enough to *discuss* it, you are not intimate enough to *have* it.

- Safe sex is mandatory. Use a condom. If you don't know this, ask someone who does. AIDS, herpes, genital warts ... yukky things lurk in this area, and so do deadly ones. A partner who doesn't care enough about you to protect your health doesn't care enough about you to have sex.

- *Don't get pregnant!* Get to know Planned Parenthood if you are having sex. This is a time when your attention should be on each other. You should be sharing and carefree, just being loved. When pregnancy is introduced into this mix, the whole dynamic changes. It is suddenly about responsibility and limited choices. A baby is a sweet gift, but if you are not ready for it, it can be an impossible burden that will eventually destroy the relationship. Take this time as a precious gift wherein you are the center of your beloved's universe.

If you are looking back at your first love, know that doing so is often helpful, especially if you seem to be having the same relationship over and over. See how your feelings during your first relationship may have set your expectations for how love was supposed to be in the future.

Remember that you will live your expectations over and over again until you change them. If you let someone treat you badly in that first relationship, odds are someone else will probably be treating you the same way in a later relationship. This is what you expect. So it will be what you attract. Often we would rather get what we expect, even if it is bad. The alternative might be:

- Taking a chance doing it another way
- Being wrong about what men or women are *always* like
- Having to learn how to have a relationship that follows a different pattern
- Hoping for something better and getting your heart broken

In the same way, if you feel you were abandoned in your first relationship, you are likely to set up conditions for abandonment over and over again. Whatever the issue is in your first experience of love, it is likely to remain the issue in your other relationships until it is dealt with and changed.

You will bring some parts of your past into your relationships, even your first one. If you were abused as a child, you are likely to choose an abuser. If you were brought up with addicted parents, you are likely to choose an addict. (And remember, alcohol is a drug; alcoholism is another addiction.) If you were abandoned, you are likely to set up abandonment in every relationship until you change your expectations.

Teen Explorations: Love, Self-Image, and the Influence of Friends

How many loved your moments of glad grace,
And loved your beauty with loves false or true,
But one man loved the pilgrim soul in you,
And loved the sorrows of your changing face.

—William Butler Yeats
When You Are Old

Apart from the first love experience and often concurrently, teenagers enter a peer group that often sets standards for whom they should love. This peer group also determines each teen's status based on looks, manner of dress, activities that are encouraged and discouraged, and many other criteria.

This is an age when we want to be more independent of our families but don't have the experience or courage to go it alone. There is thus a tremendous desire for approval from the pack. This attitude can color the choices we make for the rest of our lives if we don't change our criteria along the way.

These are also the years when we begin to form our identities in a social sense, as members of a group. These identities are determined by what other young people think of us, and our peers may judge us less by experience, generosity, and kindness than by rather superficial standards.

We also begin to determine who is a proper object of our affection by the standards of a group. In a way these people are soul mates, too, but be careful of them—they are setting up your lessons.

The things we believe are the things we will experience.

Very often this point in our lives is when we begin to form our beliefs, especially about relationships.

———

Laura began to believe as a teenager that it was the boys (later men) who knew what they were doing in a relationship. They would take the lead because they seemed to be able to remain aloof and unattached when she knew that her girlfriends were frantic for the boys. She saw boys using girls for sex and later heard them talk badly about these girls. It seemed obvious to her that the boys were controlling the process. When she married, her husband didn't really care about the marriage. She assumed that he knew what he was doing as he played indifference for power.

Later, she divorced, but she retained her assumption that it was the man who directed the relationship. She was disappointed in love over and over again.

In her forties, when her son was in his late teens and later in his twenties, Laura began to hear him and his friends talking about women. She was shocked. They didn't have any idea what was going on with girls. They obsessed about girls and then didn't call them. They believed that girls only cared about men with money and extraordinary looks. They believed that girls wanted men who treated them badly.

Clearly it was the boys who didn't know what they were doing. It took a while, but Laura finally understood that she had given her relationships up to men who barely knew how to deal with them.

————

The things we learn in adolescence can color our lives and relationships for many years if we don't go back and check the facts.

There are some really obvious ways that we make mistakes at this time. Anytime we say that any group of people is all one way or another, we are wrong. In our teenage years we may believe these generalizations because they're shortcuts for getting to understand the world. But if we keep believing that all men are this, all girls are that, or all blacks or all Italians or Yankees or Poles or Catholics or any group at all is any single thing, we are wrong.

If we believe that our value in the group will be enhanced by relationships with stars (football players, cheerleaders, or later millionaires or singers in the band), we will be looking for relationships that will never work. These relationships are not about the person but about the image.

If we attach our self-image to the kind of people we date (see above), we do ourselves a major disservice in relationship potential.

If we determine our body image by the values of peers or advertising, we can have problems with body perception for the rest of our lives. Anorexia and bulimia are illnesses, not virtues.

If you are in this stage, know that these are not the best years of your life. They are often painful, difficult years when you are finding your own way. Your friends know little more than you do. The good news is you do have a whole life ahead and can make choices and changes at any time.

———

Marcia, who weighed in at about 110 pounds and was a very pretty blonde, was told by her girlfriends from the time she was thirteen that she had a big backside. When the occasional boy would say, "That's quite a touchie," she considered this a confirmation of what her friends had told her.

As she grew up she took it for granted that she was not formed properly in that area and it was not good. But there it was, no matter how much weight she lost.

Later, when she was in her thirties, she lost a lot of weight trying to achieve the "ideal" body. But that ideal size was for a six-foot model who weighed 108 pounds, which is difficult to achieve when you are five foot two. Shortly after that several men friends explained to her that she had taken off too much weight; it was interfering with their joy in watching that part of her anatomy she had always thought to be too large.

———

If you are looking back at your teen exploration years, know that many issues in your life date to this time. If you have issues in one of the following areas, you might want to look back at this period of learning to clear them:

- The way you look is the major obstacle to feeling you are acceptable in a group.

- Your friends' opinions are more important than your own feelings when choosing a partner.
- You hold beliefs about groups of people that begin with "All" or "Only." For instance, "All girls are too emotional" or "All teachers are mean." Or "Only ugly guys date fat girls."
- You have a tendency to wear the same style of hair and clothes that you wore in high school.
- You feel that if you don't do what your friends do, you will be excluded.
- You put more value on what others think than on what *you* know to be right.
- You feel you never measure up.

The Early Twenties: Pressure to Form a Family, Tribal Influences

Your children are not your children.
They are the sons and daughters of Life's longing for itself.
They come through you but not from you.

—Kahlil Gibran

Sometime in our early twenties we begin to move out from the influence of our friends and under the influence of family. How does this happen? The need to bond and have babies is the reason.

This transition begins in the early twenties. Two by two young men and women remove themselves from the friends' group and into pairs. Young women often lead this journey, because this biological clock urges them to.

Young men have a tendency to resist, often to seek the shelter of the men's camp. One of the difficulties encountered at this time is the quality of the advice these young men tend to give to each other: It is often more appropriate to teenagers than to the real lives in which they find themselves.

At this time in life dating isn't just dating anymore; the mating dance is getting serious. This is appropriate. Young people have put the urge to form families off for five to ten years beyond the point when it would occur naturally. The twenties are the decade when the body of a woman is best suited to pregnancy and childrearing. It is time to get serious.

The kind of marriages that our culture idealizes begin at this time. If you are going to have a long partnership, it begins here, at a time when many values have been formed, but there certainly is a lot of growth ahead. If you want to share this growth in a long marriage with the natural parent of your children, this is the decade to begin.

Indeed, almost everyone who marries in their twenties expects that kind of relationship.

There is much to be said for these marriages. When everything is right, the kind of bonding and growth that are possible in a relationship that begins at this time have a different quality than those in even very good relationships that begin later. This is because we don't have much baggage yet.

There may be some parental issues or some teenage angst left here and there, but we don't usually have a bunch of kids or ex-spouses about. There is seldom property or conflicting careers to consider.

You will be able to build these experiences together—if your values are harmonious and there are no huge power issues with which you need to contend. And these shared experiences can pull the two of you together with a common goal. Each of you will come to think and feel more as the other does.

If you have a family (in the sense of parents, brothers, and sisters), this is the point from which they will be most supportive. As you follow the normal tribal patterns of forming your own family, you will find a lot of support:

- Your extended family will often help with child care and provide additional adult support for you.
- There will often be financial help with family needs—the down payment on a house, for instance.
- Family gatherings will include you and your partner as adult members that give your children a serious sense of belonging.
- There are people to talk to who have experience in family and will be pleased to share it.
- There is a very warm feeling of belonging.

There are prices to pay for this support:

- It is necessary to accept the group myth—your family's story about how they are as a family and what family means.
- You will be expected to be who your family thinks you should be.
- Family rules, values, and limitations must be observed.
- As you raise your children, you will be expected to use the sort of structure of which your family approves. This is the beginning of the socialization of the child into the community; the extended family is the original interface.

When this extended family begins to see you forming a love relationship, it quickly begins to think about marriage and children. It is the function of the family group to support this kind of growth.

Every family wants their children to have a better life than they have had. This includes the kind of romantic relationship that leads to marriage. Your parents and aunts and uncles may have had incredibly difficult times in their marriages, but in your case, they dust off all of the old romantic ideals and project them onto you.

As they do so, you will likely try to project back to them whatever you feel they need to see.

In a family with a reasonably well-adjusted past, this is not a bad thing. It is, in fact, appropriate. It is there to help you find some structure and love beyond what parents alone can provide.

Jill was twenty-two when she married and twenty-three when she had her child. From the time her son was born, families on both sides began to get involved. Holidays were big events where the families from one side or the other, or often both, would get together to eat and catch up. Her marriage to Jim was very appropriate from the perspective of an onlooker, but she wasn't happy in it. When the family got together, it seemed like everything was fine. Still, when the family wasn't around, Jill was not happy. She was lonely. Her husband did not like to be at home and used any excuse to stay away. Of course, he did not wish to discuss it.

Her son was the first grandchild and first nephew on both sides, and he just blossomed at family get-togethers with all the love and attention he received from grandparents, great-grandparents, aunts, and uncles. He was Jill's first priority and he had a big family who loved him as well.

Jill found she worked very hard for these family gatherings. She was a good cook and liked to cook for her guests. She was creative and that, too, was appreciated by the family. Her ability to focus on the larger family probably kept her in the unhappy marriage for much longer than would have been possible otherwise.

It was the World War II generation that began to break away from the traditions of staying with extended family. This is the generation that idealized family beyond its capacity to fulfill these expectations. In the 1950s, the family was painted with great sentimentality. At the same time, it began to be the nuclear family (mother, father, and children) rather than the extended family that was elevated to the real ideal.

This is when people began to think of family as a small intimate group rather than a larger clan with grandparents, aunts, uncles, cousins, and more. There were a couple of reasons for this: Returning from the war, the young men did not want to be in the position of child they held before they left. (Nor did the young women who had been working all those years.) There was also the economic reality that companies wanted workers, but they did not necessarily want them where they lived. Workers had to move from small towns to the more urban areas where the jobs were. And it was possible to move a nuclear family, but not an extended family, to the jobs.

This was effective for business, but not so good for kids. The next generation—most of whose moms went back to work—was worse off without aunts and grandmothers. And when the divorces began, the kids could have used uncles and grandfathers, but they were often a thousand miles away.

Still, when we reach our twenties, most of us find the extended family feels good again. This can be very important in finding a relationship that can last. At this point you're usually looking for a mate with similar values and experiences. Someone who fits into your family has probably had a similar beginning in life, holds similar values, and has a good chance of being able to work out a relationship with you.

Remember, if this relationship is to go long term, you need to be able to grow over the years with the same sorts of goals. You must be patient enough to support your partner's growth, and hope that your partner will know how to support yours.

If you want a long-term relationship, you have to be prepared to get through things together. And those things can be very difficult. This is a lot easier if you have the same experiences and values. These come from your family.

Those of you beginning your family life in your twenties are following the traditional path. Another group of people in their twenties will defer partnerships, though. They may get caught up in career goals or choose to travel and have some adventure while continuing their dating patterns. There is nothing wrong with this approach. But their lives will be quite different as a result. Because everyone is about to have a thirties crisis, better known in astrology as a Saturn return.

Saturn Returns: The Two Faces of the Thirties Crisis (Settle Down or Get a Divorce, Whatever You Haven't Done Yet)

The world stands out on either side
No wider than the heart is wide;
Above the world is stretched the sky,—
No higher than the heart is high.

—Edna St. Vincent Millay
Renascence

You are about to turn thirty and you wonder why you aren't happy, or why you feel so restless. You have been doing everything you thought you should, but you are not becoming who you want to be. The rules are getting old. They don't fit anymore.

This is a time when you must make changes. You might find yourself very angry with your parents at this time. If your marriage isn't working, it will not survive this crisis. The more tribal the marriage is, the more stress it will be under.

Because at this point, people move out of tribal thought and begin to become more individual.

This is a very difficult passage for a marriage. If the partnership does not honor growth, if one partner is very dominant or has been very controlling, there will be a lot of adjusting to do at this time. If the adjustment cannot be made, this is the number one time for divorces.

During the Saturn return, we are forced into growth. Anything that limits that growth will not work.

For people who have stayed single through their twenties, the change will involve taking on more responsibilities. For these people it is a big time for marriage: Change and growth mean it is time for commitment.

In a single woman the biological clock is more like a hammer now. If she is going to have a family, she knows she must get on with it. In many women, when this happens, it is a physical and emotional and probably hormonal yearning that is actually painful. When a woman needs to have a baby, she will move heaven and earth to make it so. If it hasn't happened by her thirties, priorities will change.

There are other potentials for the thirties crisis. Sometimes the wild child (who just played, maybe did some drugs and broke some laws) suddenly sees the light and goes back to school, begins a career, or becomes serious about family responsibilities. Sometimes the career drudge takes a summer off and hikes the Rockies or takes a winter and sails the Caribbean.

All of us have a strong feeling that if there was something we always wanted to do, this is the time we must begin. Nothing can get in the way; neither family nor marriage, career, old habits, nor anything can stop us.

This need to be ourselves, to discover who that is, begins with a period of time when we realize that nothing is working the way it should. Anything that has been in the way of growth will be a block now. We can't move unless we change course.

This change is not just for the sake of change. Up to this point we have been becoming socialized. This happens so that we can socialize our children and they can live in the structure demanded of them by the powers that be in their world.

By age thirty we no longer need this tribal socialization. It is time for us to begin to be the very person we were intended to be when we were born on earth. Yet these tribal forms are familiar and comfortable. Our spirits must provide obstacles right now so that we can't go on in the same way we have been going.

Spirit forces change. Often a soul mate will help you begin this process. Someone may come into your life at this time to facilitate change. This person will be very compelling. There is no way you can go on with your life as it has been if you choose to be with this person.

That may or may not mean that you have found a life mate at this time. Most often this is a transitional relationship. That does not mean that it is not an essential relationship, a blessed relationship, or an important relationship. It is all of that and more. This person has come to show you yourself and who you can become.

———

When Monica went back to college at age twenty-eight, she was at the end of her rope. Her husband had brought home a case of gonorrhea six months before. They had gone to marriage counseling and he had made promises, which he promptly forgot. She didn't know what she was going to do. She was afraid of being alone. So she decided to go back to school and prepare herself for a better job.

In a creative writing course, she began to make some friends. It was a night course, so these were people of around her age; some were undergraduates. They began going out together after class. They danced, they listened to music, they laughed and talked about writing and books they had read. It was such a compatible group that they began to call each other during the week and get together in smaller groups during the week.

Suddenly, Monica found herself having fun. She began to look forward to each day. Her husband's behavior had not improved and more and more clearly, she knew she had to do something.

She called an attorney about a divorce. She decided not to tell her husband until after it was well in progress. She began to make plans for her life, plans to be happy.

Then one night a man named Charlie joined the group. He had been in the class but remained a bit of an outsider. He came in tentatively, not really expecting to be included. He began to talk to Monica. He had caught her interest in class; he was obviously very intelligent and she liked the way he looked. Now that she began to talk to him he was absolutely compelling. He walked her back to her car and kissed her good night and the whole world changed.

They had a couple of dates the next week. She was amazed that a man could be so sensitive and intelligent. She had forgotten how wonderful it was to care about someone and to be admired by a man for more than a passing look.

The next day she spoke to her husband about a divorce. More to the point, she told him she was beginning proceedings.

The next night she had a date with Charlie. It was the first time she had enjoyed sex in five years. Her husband had been telling her that she was just frigid. When she told Charlie, they laughed until it hurt.

The divorce did not go as she planned. Her husband, who had spent five years ignoring her, suddenly decided that he was in love. It was a very difficult time for Monica. All she wanted to do now was to get on with her life; she had no feelings left for her husband. Still, he tried every means, emotional and legal, to hold her to the marriage.

Two or three times a week at first, and more as time went on, she would make up some excuse and spend time with Charlie. Sometimes she would walk into his house exhausted and he just folded her into his arms. Sometimes she was really tense; he would immediately bait her with some remark, politics or something that was going on, that made her really angry. She would find herself just screaming at him. Then he would hold her and say, "I could see you needed that. You were very angry and just holding it." She would sob in his arms and he would kiss her tears away.

Charlie loved her sarcastic side, which was coming on strong with all the stress in her life. Everybody else had always hated that about her, and she had tried to hide it for years. Charlie calmed her with music and loved her through all of it.

Eventually, Monica got her life sorted out. She found a new job and a new place to live. But her time with Charlie was limited. He had made plans for his life. She'd known this almost from the beginning. He was leaving for Europe and to another woman, a woman to whom he had made promises long before he met Monica.

When they began their relationship, Monica had thought it was probably good that it wouldn't last. It would allow her to find her own life. But as the time came when he had to go, she realized that she couldn't imagine life without him. He was part of her soul. It was agonizing that last week. It was like tearing her heart in half to see him walk to the plane.

And the first months after he left, whenever she was alone she would scream, "Charlieeee!" Maybe somewhere he could hear her.

But most of the time she spent just getting her new life together. She found new friends, found new loves. But it was a long time before in her private sad moments she stopped calling his name.

———

So often this is how a soul mate appears in your life. You need to make changes but don't know how to proceed. A soul mate comes into your life and it is suddenly clear. It is not that you do it for your soul mate; it is that you realize what needs to be done for yourself.

What sort of change can you expect at this point of your life? What is typical is a change in structure—from being who everyone else thinks you are into being your own self-actuated person. The rules must change now. The plans your parents had for your life must give way to the plans you have for yourself.

This is a time when, if you are navigating your growth appropriately, you will get angry with your parents. You are moving away from the structures they set down for you. It is all too clear to you now how these structures have held you back. Clearly you feel that your parents are to blame for hemming you in this way. The emotion of it will well up in you over and over again.

It is not a good idea to talk to them about such feelings right now. The truth is, they were doing the best they knew how to at the time. Much of this is socialization as they learned it; it came from their own parents. You may be pretty emotional about it, and that could cause you to say things that are too harsh.

Instead you might better look at the rules that you have been following all your life. Most of these came from your parents. There will also be admonitions from church, government, even your third-grade teacher. Look carefully at the rules by which you have been living.

You will find that you don't really believe in many of them anymore. You will find that others need adjustment. Still others will be simply good rules. Don't just throw away the rules you no longer believe in; change them, restructure. Put your own beliefs into your new structure. You are literally designing the rest of your life here. It must be *your* life.

The most important thing about this time is to be sure that you make the change completely. Some people see change coming and try to control it. This might work at other times of your life, but it's very detrimental now. Usually, any attempt to control change now will just make everything more intense, and you will be forced into a harder change later on. But for the person who is so strong or so stubborn that any sort of change is controlled and not completed, there are two possible consequences:

- You will not experience the growth necessary to allow you to step into the next phase of maturity.
- The energy to get into this growth will build, and your next passage (the midlife crisis) will be incredibly difficult and explosive.

The gift of the Saturn return is that if you negotiate it completely, your thirties will be much better than your twenties were. Your life will be back on track; you will finally feel that you have become the person you meant to be.

Late Thirties: Let's Do Something Completely Different

It is the things in common that make relationships enjoyable,
but it is the little differences that make them interesting.

—Todd Ruthman

With any luck and a lot of diligence, by your late thirties your life is more your own. Your career is not only on track but you have made the changes that allow you to work in a field you enjoy. You have plans to move farther along soon.

All of your friends may have changed since your late twenties. It is more comfortable now to be with people who know who you have *become* and don't identify you as the person you *were*.

There is also a tendency to break away from the tribal relationships of high school friends and family members. This doesn't mean that you just dump them. Rather, all of you have begun to find your own paths. You can't have the kind of closeness that was there when you were all in the same places in your lives.

But you have replaced those relationships with new friends who share your goals and applaud your achievements.

You have made some changes, you have made some progress. Your life is going more smoothly. You are beginning to feel that your life is your own.

Almost as soon as this is a reality, you find that there are some new issues bubbling up. You are getting bored. There is an urge to try some new things. Adventurers will want more security; emotional types will begin to take some risks. A partnership at this time serves best when it is with someone who's not like you. The TV watcher takes up with a sports fanatic and begins to ski. The world traveler needs a nester.

There are reasons for this. You have begun to see that even living your own life hasn't really given you balance. You begin to be attracted to people who bring new things into your life: partners who ground you if you are a bit flighty, or who pull you into try-ing new things if you are stuck in a rut.

Part of this is that you no longer expect that your partner will change and become more like you if he or she really loves you. You are past that now. You find that you can love people for exactly who they are. You can even love the differences between you.

Greg had always been into sports. His work was something he did to support his sports habit. He was into scuba and mountain climbing and sky diving, with some skiing and biking thrown in when he had a chance. Anything different and challenging, even a little scary, attracted him.

It turned out that he was very good at business, a natural. It was the men's-men, old-boy network to which he gravitated. With the sports he chose, he fit right in.

His relationships tended to be short lived and ended when he chose a day of sport over the woman in question.

Laura was a reader. She loved good conversation. She was an artist who was rather successful. She engaged in some sports, usually with her son, but more often a good book or a day in the garden took priority.

Greg and Laura were both in their late thirties. When they met, they talked for hours. Their lives had been so different that each was fascinated by the other.

Laura gave Greg a book. It took a while for him to read it, but he enjoyed it. He asked her to suggest another. Greg took Laura diving. She was amazed at the beauty of this new world.

As their relationship progressed, she noticed how natural he was with her son and how he brought a real sense of the mascu-line into the boy's life. Greg liked being in Laura's home, with its fresh flowers on the table and paintings on the wall. He had never given much thought to his surroundings but he noticed that it was nice to live this way.

In their twenties, neither Greg nor Laura could have appreciated each other this way. They would have argued over the differences, expecting the other to change. But in their late thirties, they could honor each other's choices and grow from the new things that each could bring to the other.

Each of them had enough confidence in who they were separately not to be intimidated by finding a new world. Rather, they found this world exciting and interesting. It was a world in which each of them could grow.

This late-thirties stage can be a gift. But if you want this gift, it is important that you have completed the growth stages that come before.

If you are still in the tribal mode, worried about what other people in your surroundings think, you will probably not be ready for this adventure. Adventure is not generally accepted in the tribe.

Laura and Greg could not have had the interesting and expansive relationship they had if they had not each brought something to it. Each of them had a life in which they had confidence, and both had found fulfillment before they even met.

Midlife Crisis

As human beings we are made to surpass ourselves and are truly ourselves only when transcending ourselves.

—Huston Smith

Just when we think we know what we are doing...at exactly the time when it looks like we can phone in the rest of our life...here comes the midlife crisis. Like the Saturn return, which psychologists call the thirties crisis, the midlife crisis is extremely well marked in astrology.

It happens when transiting Pluto squares natal Pluto—or, to put it more clearly, when Pluto has moved ninety degrees in the heavens from its position when we were born. At the moment this occurs when we reach our late thirties. Because of Pluto's elliptical orbit, though, this can vary; fifty years from now, it will occur when people reach their early fifties. Still, I'll just deal with what we have now: the midlife crisis in the late thirties to early forties.

The midlife crisis is the separation point between the first half of your life and the second. Hopefully, given the strides medical science is making, we can someday call it thirds. Traditionally it is halves, though, so we will stay with that concept.

The midlife crisis is an initiation into wisdom, and wisdom is not easily won. It may be necessary to lose a lot of baggage at this time. Some of that baggage you will have worked very hard to acquire, and you will be loathe to give it up. But if it has become baggage that keeps you from a deeper level of growth, it will go.

The midlife crisis is something that happens to you, not something you cause. It is your time for initiation to a new level of adulthood. It is not a curse, it is a gift, but it takes completing the passage to see the benefits of the thing.

A few people are either strong enough or unconscious enough not to completely experience this passage. Some control everything in their lives so much that even if the crisis begins, they won't allow it to complete its transforming work. Others are living life on such a basic level that they don't recognize anything but individual problems. Except for feeling pretty sorry for themselves, they also fail to complete the passage.

This is tragic. If there is no other really huge crisis ahead of them, these people will not grow beyond this point for the rest of this life.

This is a good time to grasp the concept of releasing attachments. Because attachments will be challenged.

When you hear this, you may be tempted to call out your devils—to say, "Take everything but..." *Do not do this.* If you do, count on it: That is the very thing you will lose.

It is a difficult passage for relationships. This and the thirties crisis are the times when most divorces happen. Any relationship whose structure will not fit the rest of your life will be tested at this time. If there is no fundamental change, the relationship will end.

It will at least end in the form it had previously. Unlike the thirties crisis, at this point relationships can often be salvaged with a separation followed by a willingness to get to know each other all over again.

This is necessary because the changes that occur now do deeply transform you. You can stay with your partner in the long run only if you both acknowledge this level of change. In many ways, the midlife crisis creates a new person.

It is important to be able to release the things that seem impossible for you to hold on to now. If they are necessary to your life in the future, you will get them back on the other side of the crisis, although they may be in a different form then.

Trying to hold on to attachments that must be released will only make this crisis more difficult. You will be trying to hold something that a force stronger than you is taking away. It can be very bruising. It is best to go with the flow and have some faith in Spirit.

Spirit is the only thing that will get you through this well—whatever you believe Spirit to be. Because this is a Pluto passage, it is about death of your old self and rebirth of a new one. This rebirth is your reward at the end of the process.

At some point, you will be so stuck in the process that you must surrender. Turn it over to Spirit. Release your control utterly. This is when the rebirth process begins.

At the other end of midlife crisis, you will feel freer than you have since you became an adult. You will know that you are wiser and you will want to reach out and help people who are themselves having a difficult time.

Just beyond midlife crisis, you may suddenly want to move, change your career, or change your friends. This is because you have become a new person. You need to have those around you relate to you as the person you have become, not the person you were. You have changed, your priorities have changed, your needs have changed. It makes sense to want to change your life now.

When you reach this point, changes no longer *just happen* to you; you choose them.

———

Roger's life was very settled. He settled for a wife with whom he was never satisfied. He settled for a job that paid rather well, but that he didn't enjoy at all. He had settled on not having children because of the ambiguities of his marriage.

Then he met Clare on the Internet. She was fifteen years younger than him and she had a life that she rather liked. She had a nice boyfriend and was planning marriage and children.

She challenged Roger's intelligence. She was just playing but he found himself being drawn in to her words. Then the dreams began. They began having similar dreams of a time long ago. It was clear that they had been together before.

She was fascinated but she was committed to her relationship, too. She and Roger also lived quite a distance apart. She didn't want to jeopardize the life she had to take a chance on a life with him. Besides, he had a wife. He didn't have anything at all to offer her.

But he was distraught. He couldn't imagine his life without Clare. Still he was afraid to change his life. Clare decided again and again to let the thing go. But he kept drawing her back with his pain.

Her boyfriend was irate about this communication. And a third man appeared in her life who seemed extremely compelling and also lived near her.

This is where they are today. How will it turn out? Will Roger take a chance and leave what he knows behind for a chance to pursue Clare? His whole life must change if he does. Or will he just feel sorry for himself and stay put, always wondering where the path might have led him?

The answer will also be the answer to his future levels of growth. Which one is the lady and which one is the tiger?

———

It is clear that Clare appeared to facilitate this midlife crisis. It is likely that if she pulls Roger into change, those changes won't lead where he expects. But the safety of the old life is killing him slowly. Will he take a chance?

If he doesn't do it of his own volition, he could find himself in a position where he both loses his life as it is and fails to win the fair maiden. Another road altogether is probably waiting for him.

But he wouldn't find that road at all if he hadn't begun this with Clare.

Some quick tips for midlife crisis:

- Let changes happen.
- Don't try to direct the thing.
- Don't call out your devils.
- Ask Spirit for help when you need it.
- Don't be afraid to surrender when it gets overwhelming.
- Let changes happen; be open to them.
- Begin to trust Spirit's help when life gets overwhelming.
- Always remember that this is part of your life's plan.
- Take six months to a year after things quiet down and try to get to know who you have become.

The Forties: Love With a Little Sense and a Few Distractions

Love does not just sit there, like a stone; it has to be made, like bread, remade all the time, made new.

—Helen Hayes

Your career is cooking right along if it ever will, and your children are getting older. They are less interested in their parents than in their friends. Parenting is not over, but a lot of the running around is.

From here on it is mostly guidance, conversation, education. Responsibilities are many, but you have learned to relax with them.

The midlife crisis has passed and you are settling into life in a new way. You are more relaxed, more philosophical. You have finally settled comfortably into your adulthood.

The biological clock has slowed its incessant beat. This has the effect of making relationships more of one-to-one, even if you both have children and live in a blended family.

Everything is mellower. In the forties it is clear to most people that they are not going to die for love. They are more accepting. They have been through a lot and understand that they bring as much baggage to a relationship as anyone. They are more tolerant.

It is common to look with concern at the changes in your face and body at this point, though. Your eyes are blurring a bit now, so you don't really notice the lines on the faces of the people you love.

Some people in their forties, in an effort to prove they are as young and attractive as ever, will find a younger lover. This has been known to work out. But most often it is an enjoyable experience that is short lived and reminds us of what we like about our contemporaries.

———

Bonnie had been dating a series of men ten to fifteen years younger than she was. In her early forties, she looked younger. The relationships were short lived but fun and she was reasonably happy with them.

Then she met Jerry. He was two years older than she was. They dated casually for a while and after a few months, they took a weekend trip to Quebec City.

They were on the point of the Frontenac, a very scenic and Old World hotel that sat above the old city and overlooking the St. Lawrence River.

The terrace had stairs that went down to the river level twenty or so long flights down. At each landing was an exit to the winding streets of the old city below. Bonnie sighed looking down.

Descending those stairs looked fascinating. She braced herself; she could do it, but it would be a lot of work.

Just then Jerry spoke. "I'll go down two levels and then we'll walk back up slowly through the streets."

Bonnie sighed in relief. Any of the younger guys she had been with would have wanted to run down and take a fast jog back up the stairs. "Oh, thank you," she said. "I am so glad you are my age."

They took a leisurely stroll through the lovely streets, took time to look at the interesting shops, and enjoyed the street entertainment over a beer.

———

You may have begun to understand that the kind of person you want in your life has changed a lot. Now you are not seeking a coparent but a partner; not a provider-nurturer but a playmate.

You have a bit more time to do things, and you can clearly see that there will be more time ahead for enjoying life. You would like to find someone who also has time to join you in exploring these things.

Then there is the baggage issue. It has been piling up through the years and it cannot be ignored now. You have become who you are by having certain opinions, interests, and ways of doing things. There is a limit to how much you can adjust.

The pool of available partners seems to have shrunk because your needs are more specific now. If you are a professional, you are not about to take a chance with a person from "across the tracks." If your life is outdoors, you are not going to enjoy someone who is allergic to trees. Certain levels of intelligence, education, and experience are simply necessary. There will be times when you are even alone doing what you do, or doing things with friends—and you will enjoy it. Once you get comfortable doing things without a date of sorts around all the time, it improves the quality of the ones who do come along.

There is a pitfall here. It is possible now to be quite happy without a relationship. If this leads to disdain for working toward relating, it could keep you from the energy of partnership for a good long time.

It is not a terrible idea. Now and then it's good to take time out from relating to get to know who you have become, to put your energy into your own life. But it can get to be so long between relationships to the point where you don't know if you want to bother with the whole thing.

At this point you may have to relearn or begin again with relationship skills before you go on. If there is a soul mate coming your way, though, he or she will find you.

Even soul mates get more interesting at this time. There are much fewer of the karmic kind. The ones who require most work have usually already made their appearance. Karma completed, this is more a time for a karmic mate, or even a twin flame who has also completed the assignment. Encountered at this point of your life, either may be simply a gift that says that you can retire together and enjoy each other's company now.

Fifties Switch: Men Want to Marry, Women Are Feeling Independent

A grown woman should not have to masquerade as a girl in order to remain in the land of the living.

—Germaine Greer

Grow old along with me!
The best is yet to be.
The last of life, for which the first was made.

—Robert Browning

I've included two quotes here, because there are two distinct points of view about operating in your fifties.

After many years of nurturing and putting off her wishes to further those of her men and children, the fifties woman begins to look around for what she is going to do now. She finds it exciting. She is finally ready to go for it.

But for the fifties man, his children are grown and he missed too much of it; his career is all it is going to be, whether it's on track or not. And he would really like to put some of his energy into a serious emotional relationship. The one he was trying to avoid in his thirties is looking very good now. After all, that's what women always said they wanted. Now he is ready. Now he gets it. So where are these women?

As you can see, the fifties stage has us fairly polarized.

There are reasons for this. Most women reach the fifties after thirty years of having to juggle and prioritize and reprioritize career, relationship, and family obligations. Then they find themselves in the hormonal passage of menopause. Once this passage is complete, they begin to want to focus on the new goals to which life has brought them.

They are not interested in compromising and giving up their goals for the benefit of someone else's. All the creativity and ambition they have been storing up, all the wisdom they have acquired, is screaming to be used. And time is flying.

It is less of a loss of interest in relationships than it is a new interest in their own lives.

Men have either reached their career goals or understand why they have not. Career is thus not as interesting as it once was. Many men look back at all those years that working took from their lives and begin to wonder what they have missed.

These are the years he planned to slow down a bit and do the things he wanted to do, and he assumed that he would have a wife who would be delighted to do that, too.

To his credit, the man has finally come to understand what women were saying all those years about a need for intimacy in relationships. He has also come to see that he could have shared more moments of his children's lives. He wants to make up for it now. Unfortunately, the children are into a busy part of their adulthood and don't really have a lot of time to offer him.

It is a sad time for a man who is becoming more aware of emotional needs. He finally gets it and they are all off having a life. There are many ways a man might respond to this development. It sometimes results in a new marriage with a younger woman and an attempt to do it all over again. Or it can lead to depression and feelings of resentment. Some men find other interests, getting very involved in a hobby that may just become a second career. And still others just try to get close to their grandbabies until everything settles down a little bit. And some work hard at finding and working out a new relationship, with the necessary compromises.

———

Alex and Jessica were happily running a small printing company while in their thirties and forties. Alex was the public person and Jessica tended to the nitty-gritty of sales and production as well as bookkeeping. As she entered her fifties, though, Jessica asked to be let out of the business to pursue her love, painting. She felt that they could hire people to do her work at the print shop so she could devote herself to painting the pictures that she had been dreaming about.

She loved just working in her studio. Her skill developed, and soon she had a gallery show. Its success felt like her first victory. She was on her way—until Alex told her he was going to sell the print shop and look for a new career. In the meantime, he would manage her career so that she could focus on her art.

Soon he had her traveling around the country to shows. Her work was selling faster than she could produce it. Now she was choosing subjects because other people wanted a painting of this or that. She was making money, but it was always a struggle. And the joy of the art was getting left behind with all the obligations she faced.

Alex was doing less and less. She asked him to find some work he would enjoy to help her support them so that she could get back to focusing on her art. That was when Alex began getting sick. It was nothing particular, just a series of little illnesses and injuries that kept him from working. The bills ran up.

Alex, for his part, was afraid. The print shop went downhill after Jessica left, and it made him lose his confidence about working on his own. He couldn't hire good people for minimum wage. When he went above minimum wage and added benefits, he could no longer compete with his competitors' prices. He sold the business when it was at its weakest. Alex had no confidence in himself as a businessman.

He thought that he was being an "enlightened male" by working as a support person for his wife. Jessica, however, felt that he was sabotaging her dream.

Alex had acquired a knowledge of personal computers in the print shop. He had been on the Internet early and, as his friends began to jump on, helped them set up Web pages. Then he began to design a page for selling Jessica's art. With his new knowledge, he could do more to help friends with their attempts to reach out to Internet commerce.

Soon he had a little design business of his own. The illnesses were getting in the way of his interests, and gradually they stopped. He began to exercise more.

Jessica painted more and traveled less. Alex got an office outside his home for his growing business.

This is one of the thousands of ways that the fifties can work out. This stage is just beginning to be rewritten by the baby boom generation that has led the way in all of the changes our social and cultural structure has been undergoing. It remains to be seen what this decade will become in the future.

The Sixties: Not Yet Rewritten

*To know how to grow old is the master work of wisdom, and
one of the most difficult chapters in the great art of living.*

—Henri Frederic Ameil

The sixties as they have been and as they will be are two different things. We are on the edge of a change in the tone of this life
stage because of the medical advances that are so quickly changing the process of aging. The potential already exists for us to be
physically healthy and youthful well into our seventies.

Adding better health to lives that have already acquired knowledge and experience will completely change the dynamic of the
decade.

As usual, the baby boom generation will redefine the genera-
tional change, as will the technology of medicine that keeps us
healthier longer and longer. As this generation approaches its sixties, there is every chance that for the first time in history, its
members will be as robust as they were in their forties. This alone
will make for some satisfying golden years. And chances are that
we will not live these years the way our parents did.

It is doubtful that we will want to carry on and keep doing the
same job we always did. Doubtful, too, that we will spend these
years golfing and vacationing.

It will be interesting to see what happens as we enter this
uncharted territory as healthy and intelligent adults. Without a
doubt, there will be a new kind of karmic drama available at this
time—one that can include, as in no other decade, a highly
evolved soul mate.

PART THREE

FINDING YOUR SOUL MATE

Do you want me to tell you something really subversive?
Love is everything it's cracked up to be. That's why people
are so cynical about it. It really is worth fighting for, being
brave for, risking everything for. And the trouble is, if you
don't risk anything, you risk even more.

—Erica Jong

There is nothing like love. It is literally a drug when you begin, not unlike chocolate. We all want to find it and to keep it new. Perhaps if we find our soul mate this will happen. Perhaps.

After a few weeks, the drug stabilizes and you have to deal with the reality of the relationship. It's not that the drug never returns; it just seldom comes back with the same rush of intensity it had at the beginning.

In reality, the best you can do is to find a soul mate who wants and intends to consciously participate in your life at its highest level. Someone who is himself or herself evolved beyond the games and expectations of socialization. Someone who can grow with you and play with you and be serious, when it is time for that. But this person must feel just right to you. If you have to force yourself to care about someone, that someone is not a soul mate. A soul mate will touch your heart effortlessly.

Remember that your soul mates come to participate in your growth. The more you are already into a state of growth, the greater the chances of that meeting taking place. The more you examine your life, the more you love yourself, and the more you expect the best, the likelier becomes the possibility of meeting a soul mate of the highest order.

Releasing Attachments—Letting Love Come In

Forgiveness does not change the past, but it does enlarge the future.

—Paul Boese

We all walk through life with emotional baggage. Don't blame yourself, don't blame your partner, don't blame your mama. Blame is about the most counterproductive thing you can do in any circumstances. It makes you a victim.

The way to stop being a victim is to take total responsibility for your own life.

The single exception I will grant to this principle is for abused children. Children are not capable of taking responsibility for their own lives and thus are seriously wronged when the adults they depend upon become their abusers.

But on the bright side, there are lots of people now who are trained to help you work through the residue of old abuse and clean it up once and for all. As an adult you can choose not to be victimized by your past anymore.

Is it painful? For a while; you have to touch the pain to heal it properly. But most abusers would have the effects of the abuse surgically removed in a minute, if it were possible. Therapy is much less an ordeal than that. And when your work is done, you are healed.

When we are dealing with karma, we need to know that each person who passes through our lives is a gift and a lesson. Sometimes they are carefully disguised and appear to be very bad people. But they only do what we allow them to do. Once we learn the lesson, we do not need to allow the old energies to guide us any longer.

Until the lesson is learned and the experience is released, we will often find the same lesson appearing in different clothes over and over again. This is why it is important to understand what the past has brought us in relationships and to forgive them (because they were teachers) and to release them (because we no longer need that lesson).

Unless the energy has been cleared and released, most of us have a fair amount of baggage. This has manifested as:

- Emotional disappointments
- Abandonment issues
- A series of bad relationships
- Deeply held negative beliefs

There are many techniques that will allow us to let go once and for all of that kind of emotional baggage.

And the greatest of these is forgiveness.

We do not forgive to release the other party of responsibility. We forgive to release ourselves of the burden of sadness or anger or hatred. All of these emotions are too heavy to bear for your whole life. Forgiving helps you to release them and be rid of them once and for all.

Because there is always a bit of guilt related to these feelings, it is best to forgive yourself twice for every time you forgive someone else.

You may have to do this meditation more than once. You need to take some time with it.

Begin by finding a place where you can be alone and not interrupted. Take ten cleansing breaths. (Breathe in very deeply and release the breath slowly.) As you release the breaths, feel yourself becoming more and more relaxed. Let the exhaling breaths release any tension you are holding in your body.

From this relaxed position, picture yourself in strength in a safe, beautiful place. One by one see all the people whom you love and who have loved you join you in a big circle. They are all around you supporting you with unconditional love. Let go of any old issues

*with these people; know that they are there because they love you
and want to help you in this time of growth.*

*Now picture the one who needs forgiveness walking into that cir-
cle of love and holding a hand out to you. Picture the person asking
your forgiveness.*

*Feel the feelings that come over you now. You understand how
you have been hurt. But you also see that the other person was only
being what he or she knew to be. In this circle of love, it is easy to
understand and to forgive. You watch as the energy of this person
slowly fades from the circle and releases itself. You are left surround-
ed by friends and loved ones.*

*Let yourself feel the relief of releasing all of the old hurt and anger;
feel the old emotions dissipate. Let yourself feel the love that the universe and your circle of love within it provide to you every day.*

*In this spirit, holding this openness to love, take three cleansing
breaths and slowly find yourself back in the present, feeling lighter
and happier than you have in a long time.*

You can do this forgiveness exercise as many times as you need to
release long-held emotions.

It is not necessary, in fact it might be counterproductive, to tell
the other person that you have forgiven. If this person has not
moved to a higher point of understanding, more resentment could
result if you recount your forgiveness. It could start the whole
negative process again. It is not worth it.

Once you feel that you have released the old emotions and
learned the lessons from your past relationships, then you can
begin to look to the future, expecting something better.

What to Really Look For

*The mind I love must have wild places, a tangled orchard
where dark damsons drop in the heavy grass, an overgrown
little wood, the chance of a snake or two, a pool that
nobody's fathomed the depth of, and paths threaded with
flowers planted by the mind.*

—Katherine Mansfield

Fortunately, different people like different kinds of mates! Certain
qualities make certain kinds of mates more desirable or even possible in one part of your life than in another. For instance, a person
with a background similar to yours might make a really good partner to raise your children with, but later on you might prefer
someone a little more adventurous.

It is always best to find a partner who genuinely likes the opposite sex—a woman with men who are friends, a man with women
friends. Communication is always better with people like this. And
they are more likely to think of you as an individual, rather than
just a woman or a man.

A similarity of backgrounds or values makes relating easier. But
if you happen to be attracted to the exotic, you will just need to
cultivate more communications skills, and learn to accept and even
relish the differences. Those differences can keep life interesting.

Certain things will make a relationship better. They sound simple, but the skills to make a relationship work can take a long time
to acquire. If you are looking for a partner who might have
acquired these skills, look at his or her relationships. Not only the
romantic ones—the friendships and the family relationships will
also show you a lot about a person's relationship skills.

Since most of us come from families that were dysfunctional in
some way, we must not jump to conclusions about anyone whose

family life was not perfect. Indeed, the ones who show very strong forms of family attachment are as often as not masking some very bad family dynamics. So don't be too judgmental here. Should you be lucky enough to find a partner whose family was mostly functional, and who still shares warm relationships with them, you have a partner who is likelier to have some developed relationship skills.

Another quality that will point to these skills is friendships. Men's friendships and women's friendships are different, but if you see genuine warmth and concern in the interaction between friends, then you've found people with a real capacity for relationships.

You will want a reasonable match in intelligence and sensitivity in a partner, too. If her idea of intelligent company is someone who keeps up with politics and his idea is keeping up with the latest in quantum mechanics, it may or may not be a mismatch. Yet if his ideas of a good time is catching big bass and her idea is the theater...maybe they should think again.

Things sometimes work out between a fisherman and a sophisticate, but only if other solid areas of interest overlap.

Oddly, these things are often overlooked when the chemistry is feeling right and the nights have been lonely. And maybe you *could* learn to fish. But don't marry him until you know.

All of this, however, depends on some very logical assumptions about what relationships should be. But what about the partner who clearly rings your bells, yet is not logically the best choice you can make? If you are looking for a soul mate, your feelings can be a giveaway that something is important for you here. Don't let your logic overrule your heart every time. Often the heart knows that there is more to a relationship than meets the eye.

Perhaps she is your next teacher...perhaps he is your next spouse. It needs to be explored.

A Few Serious Don'ts

How come dumb stuff seems so smart while you're doing it?
—Dennis the Menace

There are a few absolute bottom lines in relationships. There are some people who simply cannot have a relationship back with you no matter how hard you try. Don't expect that you can have a normal relationship with the following:

- People with addictions. It can be an illegal drug or a legal one; alcohol is just another drug. It is addiction when it affects someone's life.
- People with mental illnesses. Unless they are being treated and cooperating with the treatment, they just cannot be a committed partner in a relationship. Mental health is a bottom line that you must have for a reasonable relationship.
- Very controlling or obsessive people.

These are mostly not bad people; they are simply too involved with their own difficulties to be capable of relating back to you in any sensible way. If you feel you must be in relationships with people in these categories, do not expect that you can change them. They simply cannot focus their energies on relating to you. They can love you, they can need you, they can be compelling, but they can't relate.

In the case of very controlling people, there is always the chance of it escalating to an abuse situation. This is heightened if you have experienced abuse in your past. You need to work through and heal that area of your life before you get into another relationship, because if you don't, chances are that you will choose another abuser.

If you are with and addict, you must be aware of the flip side of this issue—codependency. Codependency is a series of behaviors that actually facilitates an addiction. It includes all the things you do to ignore the addiction and all the things you do to enable it. For example, consenting to be the victim or the victimizer, or always taking your partner back no matter how bad the behavior might have been, are codependent behaviors. You can't help your partner if you feed into the addiction this way. There are books and groups that can help you with this issue. If you are one of these people, get to know them.

Often the people who are attracted to addicts have had this issue for their entire lives. Addictive parents and lovers appear in their stories over and over. These are the folks who can swear off addicts (or alcoholics) and decide to date only people from the strictest church in town. And of course still come away in love with the only addict there.

Only changing the codepedency can help this, not reforming a series of addicts. As a matter of fact, a reformed addict would no longer hold any charm for a codependent until that issue is healed. A codependent needs an addict as much as an addict needs a codependent.

Some Thoughts About Need

In less enlightened times, the best way to impress women was to own a hot car. But women wised up and figured out it was better to buy their own hot cars and then they wouldn't have to ride around with jerks.

—Adam Scott

There is a metaphysics about need. This is often the reason we feel pulled toward a relationship beyond the physical needs of the sex drive. Because we are in this dimension of time and space to learn and grow through a series of lives, there have also been times between lives when we have felt the comfort of another reality.

In this reality, when we don't have bodies to separate us, we can feel the presence and interconnectedness of all of the cosmos as though it was a part of us. We know our divine connection intimately.

Then we chose to reenter the physical limitations of life and we find that we are separate again. Alone in our own skin. It is this separation that makes us long for the profound connection a soul mate can bring. Soul mates are our larger family.

The reality, though, is that each of us *is* alone in our own skin in this life. Even the intensity of a sexual connection with a beloved soul mate can only take that separation away for moments.

The need for connection is profound and exists in every soul on this planet. It is so deep that politics, commerce, and religion have taken that need and exploited it to add to their own power.

That has led to the current myth of neediness and loneliness and fear.

The interests of the churches, the state, and advertisers are different. But all promote their agendas by addressing our fears. And the fear of loneliness is especially exploited. It is easier for these institutions to manage a populace of needy codependents than it is to manage confident, secure individuals.

It is in the best interest of the powers that be in this world to keep us in need and fear.

Because we have a need for connection coupled with a very intense sex drive, the whole business of relationships can easily be manipulated. So you will find that there is a great deal of social pressure for you to think about relationships in ways that are not productive, much less powerful.

The structures that make up our society are not served by a confident, self-actuated populace.

Taking Responsibility for Your Choices

*Each of us makes his own weather, determines the color of
the skies in the emotional universe which he inhabits.*

—Bishop Fulton J. Sheen

When you can understand that you've made mistakes and not beat yourself up for it but learn the lesson and persevere, then you are ready to make your life what you want it to be.

Much of what you have been taught all your life is not true. You do not need to be victimized. You do not need to just respond to life. You have the power to direct your life and your relationships.

But you can't do this if you spend any time assigning blame or feeling like a victim. If you want to have this kind of power, you must take responsibility for your whole life. If he did you wrong, well, you let him. You can choose not to let anyone do that to you again. If you look at the situation, you'll realize that you saw the warning signals and chose to continue anyway.

"Oops, sorry, my fault, I picked a loser and let him stay even after I knew about it. I screwed up, sorry life" is a more powerful statement than, "All the men I meet are controlling and they all cheat." Or, "I chose another woman who was looking for a man with money" is more powerful than, "All women are looking for money and if they find someone with more money they will leave me."

If you stay in the mind-set that insists you are a victim of fate, then fate will prove to you over and over again that you are just that. It is because you haven't yet learned the lesson that you can choose. Until you learn this lesson, life will keep sending you teachers to say, "You didn't get it last time, let's try it again."

One soul mate after another will come to you disguised as the kind of victimizer you have consistently chosen. This is not to punish you, it is to encourage you to take the step that will change everything: taking responsibility for the kind of relationships in which you have been allowing yourself to be involved.

If your relationships have been toxic, why have you been in them? Because you think that they happen to you. The reality is that you chose them. You can choose not to go that way anymore. If you find that you are happier alone than with him, he isn't good for you. If you think you can't be alone, it is time to learn.

When you can be alone and be happy, you will always know that you can chose relationships and set limits in them. Then the only downside to ending a relationship is that you are alone again—and you know it is fine to be alone. This is power.

You have choices. It is your responsibility to find a relationship that is happy and conducive to growth. It is also your responsibility to choose not to be in a toxic relationship.

Taking responsibility opens up a world of potential in relationships. You can, for instance, chose to get involved with someone just because she's fun. It's not that you intend to be involved with her long term—just for the moment and just because you need a little fun right now.

You can spend time with people who are quite different from you in age or background just to find out what it is all about. It becomes unnecessary to prequalify everyone at a potential mate.

Once you are meeting people because you are interested in them as people and not as potential coparents, you will find that you won't stay in a relationship if it does not meet your needs. You will be able to begin and end relationships with more ease and less hurt feelings. This will begin to build confidence.

It is into a life like this that a soul mate is most likely to appear.

When you are stuck in the victim rut, you almost force people to victimize you. You behave as you have when you felt victimized in earlier relationships. You don't take responsibility for the relationship; you assign it all to your partner. And worst of all, you begin to expect that you will get the same kind of relationship again. This, of course, draws the same energy into your life over and over again.

The victim is as much a part of a victimizing relationship as the victimizer. This is similar to the codependent relationship. You may have seen a victim-victimizer relationship in your parents' marriage; these roles are often learned in childhood. But many things are learned in childhood that can be changed when you become an adult. If you take the responsibility.

So often we find ourselves in a relationship because we think that the other will be able to meet some vague emotional needs of ours and make us feel whole. In reality this is something we must do for ourselves.

No one else can be responsible for our own healing and wholeness. Since most of us would like to have a partner who is healed and whole, then it is our responsibility to present them with as complete an individual as we can manage.

If you are responsible for your own life, you can try new things. You don't need to repeat patterns that were not productive; you are still free to make new choices. Other people cease to have the ability to keep you from your dreams. You are free to do what you need to do to make them come true.

A Few Things to Consider

We cannot live for ourselves alone. Our lives are connected by a thousand invisible threads, an along these sympathetic fibers, our actions run as causes and return to us as results.

—Herman Melville

As you seek your soul mate, there are a few points that you want to be careful about. First, be sure to ask for someone who wants you exactly the way you are.

Second, it is very important not to try to change someone else's destiny. If you do this it will not go well for you. There is in Wicca the Rule of Three: What you put out will come back to you threefold. Anytime you are trying to make a conscious change in destiny, keep this in mind. Make sure that what you are putting out there is what you think it is.

You may think that you are putting love out toward someone when you are actually trying to control his life and change his destiny. This will not have good results. Even if you get what you asked for, it can backfire.

It is always better to ask for the right person to come into your life than to ask that a specific person come in. The one exception is if you have a pretty good idea that the person wants to be there.

Another thing you want to avoid is calling a "come here" to members of your karmic family. Because they will hear you, and they will interrupt the lives they were meant to have to join you— but they are not supposed to be in your life at that time, and they cannot stay. so you will feel that connection and bond with them and they will have to go. You will then have to miss them for the rest of your life. It really is better and easier on your heart not to do this.

The last admonition I will give you is not to use a past-life connection to try to make people do what you want them to do in this life. It is not fair, it is not appropriate and it is bad manners. Besides, it does not work.

Visualizing and Manifesting

Reach high, for stars lie hidden in your soul.
Dream deep, for every dream precedes the goal.

—Ralph Vaull Starr

Here is how you can change your life. This is the technique that will bring the person you need into your life. It definitely works. But remember: *Be careful what you ask for, for you will surely get it.*

So before we get into the technique, it is necessary to take some time to do it correctly.

Take Stock

The first thing you need to do is to learn to value yourself. Without this, you will not allow yourself to require the best or most appropriate partner for yourself. You need to know that you have qualities that are worthwhile and that will attract the partner you really want.

So make a list of your own fine qualities. Here is are some particulars that may or may not apply to you; use what applies and feel free to add others.

Cute	Playful	Sweet	Creative
Caring	Emotional	Extravagant	Experienced
Careful	Intelligent	Sensible	Down to Earth
Handsome	Generous	Neat	Reserved
Gentle	Daring	Social	Spiritual
Elegant	Thrifty	Well educated	Enthusiastic
Strong	Fun loving	Independent	Intellectual
Smart	Sexual	Cultured	Homebody
Graceful	Cuddly	Demonstrative	
Beautiful	Logical	Athletic	

It is important that you write the truth. Once you have done this, you should be able to see clearly why the perfect person for you would want you to be in his or her life. When you see yourself on paper, you will see that you have plenty to offer a person who shares your values.

Because you have many soul mates available to you, it is necessary to find the one who suits your life as it is today. The perfect person for a twenty-year-old might be very wrong for the forty-year-old person you have become. So think in terms of where you are today and what you need for growth in your life right now.

Think, too, about what really makes you happy, not what you think should make you happy. If you really don't like to stay home but think you should settle down, don't think that a settled mate will make you happy. If you have always loved having pets, don't overlook the fact that a person who does not like animals is not for you.

Think of the things you need in your life to make you happy, and be specific in expecting a mate with those qualities that will support your happiness.

So Make a List of What You Need

Think hard about what makes you happy. Think hard about what qualities you will need in a partner. Think about what qualities will not be acceptable, too. The biggest animal lover in the world will not do if she is also an addict.

My own list might look like this:

Intelligent	Spiritual
Witty	Good grammar
Tall and slim	Sensitive
Educated	Sensual
Well read	Honest
Animal Lover	Sane
Comfortable amount	Not adddicted
of money	Has cleaned up his childhood
Confident	issues
Not controlling	Has good women friends
Affectionate and sexual	Happy in his life
Physically active	Adventurous
Nature lover	

Make the list as long as you want. Go back and add things as you think of them. Don't worry about getting too choosy or specific. If there are qualities that don't work for you, add them in a separate column.

If you really want a millionaire, don't ask for somebody who just has a job. But remember the sorts of things having a millionaire mate may require of you and ask yourself if you want to make those changes. For instance, what would it do to your friendships? Would you be comfortable with his friends?

If you are only attracted to dark-haired people, add this to the list. You should be attracted to your soul mate if the relationship is to have a potential to make you happy. Nothing that matters to you is too small or too silly to consider. It is possible that you have been attracted to that kind of person all of your life because your intuition has told you that your soul mate would have these qualities.

Think long and hard about these things. You are more likely to have your life lessons around some little thing you forgot to add or something you asked for that has a lot of other issues attached than from not getting what is on your list.

Make Another List

Now list every reason why you don't think you can have such a person come into your life.

One of the reasons why you don't have such a relationship now is that you are convinced that it is not possible for you, for one reason or another. Now is the time to explore what is keeping you from it: your own beliefs.

A belief that women will abandon you will lead you to attract women who can't commit. A belief that people who have enough money will never like you acts as a money repellent. If you find yourself saying that there are no good men or women left in your city, then your search is doomed to fail.

Your belief in your own unworthiness is keeping you from making connections more than any real limitation.

Your list may have some of the following beliefs...but is not limited to them:

I am not good looking enough.

I am too fat (thin, tall, short, dark, light, freckled, ugly, gorgeous) to be attractive to the kind of person I really want.

I am not smart enough.

I am not interesting.

I am too quiet (loud, bossy, naive, weak , strong, stupid, brilliant).

Nobody likes a shy person (loudmouth, et cetera).

I don't have enough money (a house, a car, a horse, a retirement account, stocks).

Women only look for men with lots of money.

Men are only attracted to beautiful women.

Women don't like short men (tall men, fat men, bodybuilders, bald men, blond men, dark men).

Men don't like short women (tall women, fat women, body-builders, blond women, dark women).

Some of these beliefs may seem silly to you, when you think about them, and some of them may seem sensible. The truth is that none is a good enough reason to keep someone who loves you away. Before you can draw what you want into your life, you must change these core beliefs. It is not beneficial to try to go back and understand why you hold them. It is not important. What is important is that you know:

- That you are a beloved part of the interconnectedness of all things, and the universe supports you.

- That however you think of the identity of the divine—God, Goddess, or Spirit—it is participating personally in your opportunities for growth.

- That you are a personally lovable human being and people are waiting to come forward in your life to show you that.

- That the only thing you need to do to change your life is to know that you can, and to believe and act as though the change has already been made.

Say the Magic Words

You can clearly see that you should change your beliefs. So now they should follow. Right?

Well, they don't. They don't because they are stored well below the rational part of your brain. They have become firmly entrenched and cannot be reprogrammed by thought or logical decisions.

You have to get to these places with repetitions. This is the same way your mother did when you were little, and your girl-friends did when you were in your teens, and so did your third-grade teacher, along with all the other people and institutions in your life that have added beliefs into your brain.

That is why you keep hearing about affirmations. They sound silly, even embarrassing. After all, you have been taught not to brag about yourself . You have been taught to use your rational mind to make changes in your life. The very people who used rep-etitions to program your beliefs have taught you this.

So it is time to learn the magic words, and how to use them.

An affirmation is a positive statement in the present tense. It's not an "I will have…" statement; those always stay in the future and never get into your present life. You must put the affirmation in the present tense so that when it has cleared your old beliefs and added new ones, it's true in the present.

"I am attracting the man or woman of my dreams" is a good all-purpose affirmation for attracting love. But before we get to that one, let's clear up some negative areas.

Try this one: *"The man or woman of my dreams loves everything I am."* Or *"My soul mate loves the person I really am."*

Speak your affirmation out loud ten times. You will notice lots of little negative thoughts creeping in. They will be telling you all the reasons that this affirmation is not true and cannot possible work for you. These are the little thought-devils that have been keeping you from your dreams.

So line them up. Put them on paper. Make another list. As fast as you can, keep writing them down. As more come, write those. Repeat the affirmation when they slow down and watch as more come up. Write all of it down on paper. Keep doing this until the thought-devils stop or are repeating themselves.

Look at that piece of paper. Look at each item Do you believe those things? Many of them have come directly from beliefs that other people have put into your head. Many of them are from a different time in your life. Many are not true at all. Look carefully at them: These are the things that are stopping you from meeting the person who will really be good for you. They are the ten-foot-high stone fence between you and a happy relationship. But that fence is not stronger than you, so tear it down. Blow it up if you must. Or just take it apart small stone by small stone. It is your choice and your style.

Carry that piece of paper around with you for a couple of days. Keep the pencil too, so that when more of the little devils pop up you can capture them on the paper. Keep repeating your affirmation.

It took many years for you to develop these negative thought patterns...these devils. It may take a couple of weeks to change these patterns. But stay with it; don't let one of them remain unchallenged.

When you are pretty sure that you have eliminated the thought patterns around this affirmation, ceremoniously burn your list of devils. Choose a full moon to do this. For the next two weeks relax with the knowledge that you are preparing to find your soul mate. On the new moon, begin your new affirmations.

Speak each affirmation seven times and repeat this at least seven times a day.

List of Affirmations

My highest soul mate is coming into my life now.
My beloved loves me just the way I am.

I have everything I need to attract the love of my life.

I trust the universe to send me the highest and best soul mate.

As I love myself more, my soul mate comes lovingly into my life.

I am lovable and deserve love in my life.

I honor all the love in my life and so attract my soul mate effort-lessly.

My soul mate sees my beauty and honors the goodness of my heart.

I am without need and full of love for the soul mate who is about to enter my life.

My soul mate is ready to enter my life now.

I am exactly the person my soul mate will love.

Close Your Eyes and See—

Close your eyes, take a couple of deep breaths, and relax completely. Using the list of characteristics you made earlier, visualize the soul mate you would like to enter your life now. Remember to give him or her all the qualities that you put on the list. Picture that person moving around in your home. Picture what his or her home would look like. When you are happy with the picture, add one thing to it. Add a marker.

The marker can be a color or an object. It's simply what you will notice when you meet this person that tells you this is indeed what you have called into your life.

Surround your vision with clear white light and watch it float away into the universe. Now let it go. It is out there preparing and manifesting for you. Don't worry about it. Have confidence that this is the experience the universe will bring to you.

Do not attach any need to this image; do not attach any fears. If you do you will only manifest neediness and fear. Just let it go in the knowledge that it is out there getting ready to come into your life.

There is no need to make it happen. It is no help to feel neediness for it; in fact, that might push it farther out as your needs—which become your beliefs—manifest.

While you are waiting to have this visualization manifest, fill your days with the things you love. Let the love that is already there come in. Children, pets, gardens, friends, relatives…whatever you give love to. Know that it is being returned. Love is what you should focus on. Don't be afraid to love lavishly.

If you don't feel you have enough resources for love, then look around for people you can help. Help out of love and feel the love pour back in. The more you immerse yourself in love, the more you magnetize it to you.

Love is love. It is not worth any less or more from pets or children or your mother than it is from a soul mate, for indeed, they are your soul mates too.

Give thanks every day for the love you do have. Give thanks for the love that is coming to you. Don't whine. Don't feel sorry for yourself. Don't yearn.

Yearning brings yearning. Love brings love.

Where to Meet: Things That Work

If it is your time, love will track you down like a cruise missile.

—Lynda Barry

Soul mates will find you, given half a chance. I have seen cases where they actually came and knocked on the door, though this is rare. You will have better luck finding yours if you in fact get out of the house.

Because soul mates are part of your karmic family, meeting them through your own family connections or those connections that feel like family is often the best choice. Spending time with family or close friends will often widen your circle of friends to include their friends and, eventually, friends of friends.

Widening circles is the way you meet people. The first level is the people you meet directly, the second is their friends, the third (and so on) the friends who wander into the circle through the widening levels.

But most people want to find their soul mate with a first-level meeting. Maybe it's because we live at such a fast pace today that we try to minimize social time into something "productive."

This might work in business, but even there most of us realize that we need to form a network. Why should finding your soul mate be somehow more direct?

This network can be formed almost anywhere. You can start with people who are already your friends; you can start with your family and their friends. You can start from a group that shares your interests. You can start pursuing new interests.

Mostly you need to become more active. Be friendly; remember that most of the people you meet are also trying to meet others, and are very afraid of rejection. If you can help them relax, you will have friends.

And remember to reject rejection. If you run across someone who doesn't have social skills enough to be polite, don't let that lack of taste and poise reflect on your feelings of self-worth. Sadly, there are quite a few people who don't bother to learn social skills. They should not be the ones by whom you measure yourself.

If you are pursuing interests in order to meet people, it is important to really get into the interests themselves. The people who share these interests will then have things in common with you.

————

Julie was newly divorced and wanted to meet some single people. She decided that skiing might be a way to do this. She had just begun skiing and enjoyed it. So every Friday she went to the slopes and fought her way down the bunny slope then back to the lodge to hopefully meet men. She met no one.

But she started trying to ski a little bit faster. She took a few lessons. She tackled more difficult slopes. She was beginning to love the sport. She signed up for a ski trip to Vermont. On the bus she met other skiers. They were better than she was, they had been skiing for years, but she decided to try skiing with them. It was fun, but she had to push herself. She had never had so much fun. After skiing they enjoyed meals together and dancing.

Back home, they kept in touch. She took two more trips that winter. On one of them, she met Jon through her friends. They talked all that evening and skied together the next day. On the bus going home, they made plans to see more of each other.

———

If Julie had stayed on the bunny slopes, she would not have made the connections that brought her to this new romance. Sometimes we must push ourselves harder to achieve certain goals. Julie's experience is a case in point.

Another way to meet people is to get into community activities. You can work through your church or any of the volunteer groups that always welcome help. The people you work with there will share your values, and you will meet them naturally in the course of your own work. In the meantime you will have done something worthwhile.

Sharing the love of a sport or activity is part of the connection; you can't fake it. If you have to fake it, you have chosen the wrong path. Imagine finding someone who is passionate about a sport or activity that bores you. You would not enjoy that encounter. You need to find interests you can honestly share.

When you find something you really enjoy, you will find people who like to share it—and you will have opened up your life to a new source of joy besides.

Some Things Women Should Know About Men

*A man falls in love through his eyes, a woman through
her ears.*

—Woodrow Wyatt

Men and women are different in so many ways. While this is usually part of what we like about each other, it sometimes it drives us nuts. You need to understand the differences that aren't so obvious in order to understand what it is the other gender values.

First consider this. Men naturally understand power; women naturally understand emotions. This doesn't mean that men don't have emotions and that women know nothing about power. It means that these are our natural arenas. Of course there are many levels between these two poles, but power is usually the first thing a man will check out in a situation, and emotion is what a woman will sense.

This is deeply ingrained; it goes back to the dawn of humanity and beyond. Animals that live in troops, tribes, or packs organize themselves socially in this way. The males work within a hierarchy that depends on strength and intelligence and posturing. An alpha male is the leader of the males in that particular pack. A male that is banished from the pack has very little chance of survival.

Females also have a hierarchy but it revolves more around caretaking than around power. It's a much subtler hierarchy determined by emotional instincts.

And even though we humans are all sophisticated and intelligent and even beginning to move into outer space, we can still look around at groups of men and see the same posturing that occurs in wolf packs and gorilla troops.

But the truth is, if you want a man you'd better try to understand.

When a man enters a roomful of other men he will automatically begin to rank them: who is alpha, who is up, who is down. Men really have a sixth sense about these things.

But one of the things you need to know that nobody mentions is that the woman a man chooses has everything to do with his perception of his own power.

When a woman feels insecure, she says, "I'm fat." When a man feels insecure he says, "My girlfriend is fat."

This old joke says a lot about how a woman projects the public image of a man. The whole reason a wolf fights to become the alpha male is so that he can earn the right to mate with the alpha female. This assures that the strongest wolf genes are passed on to future generations. Men have an instinct very similar.

Men fight to become alpha by earning money, or excelling in sports, or piling up honors in their field, or finding a position of power. Once they have achieved alpha status, they seek an alpha female.

Should a man acquire an alpha female before he has actually earned alpha status, he will typically feel that she adds to his perceived status and makes him more likely to be ranked highly in the hierarchy.

When men are quite young, their perception of which women are alpha centers on how the women look. To acquire alpha status a woman must be close to the ideal in looks. This ideal seems to have everything to do with slimness, perhaps with height, and with style. Young women measure themselves and their self-worth against this ideal at an age before true accomplishment is possible.

This push toward alpha status is extremely strong in the young. It is a biological function that ensures that the strongest genes survive for the future. The need to be popular often seems like life or death to young people. It is why some women will starve themselves and feel completely unworthy if they are not slim enough. Slimness is nothing but current style; look at alpha females of the past and you will see a lot more roundness.

Now, not all men will become alpha. Indeed, most of them will not. But any man will then take whatever ranking he has earned and try to increase it by the female partner he chooses.

Many of the men who do not become alphas merely mellow

out and find a lot of happiness in their lives. They make good parents and good partners. Others remain restless; they feel that they got less than they deserved in this life.

It is usually when he reaches his thirties that a man must come to terms with his position in the ranks. Some men who are not particularly competitive drop back in their teens or twenties and try to just have a life. But even the alphas come to a moment when they must give up their rank to a younger and stronger generation.

These are issues that women often don't consider. And for some reason very little relationship advice includes this information.

As a woman you have to decide what kind of man suits you. Many women would in fact be very happy to be with a dropout from the ranking. But those women are often convinced that they should have done better.

This is because in human history, the ranking of a woman has most often come from the reflected ranking of the man she is with. This is not always so in the animal world; still, it is the message we get from society as a whole.

And because of this message, choosing a mate who has opted out of the whole business of ranking—even if he is the very best partner for you—can seem like dishonoring yourself in some vague way. Many women will choose an alpha wannabe rather than being happy with an unranked partner.

Another issue is what field a man is ranked in. Different women appreciate different arenas. For instance, if you see sports as the hero arena, then a businessman, no matter how strong he is in his field, will not strike you as an alpha. Even a millionaire might seem like kind of a wimp. And conversely, if money is your marker for an alpha, then a jock won't do it for you.

If you feel that you need an alpha male, be prepared for some realities:

Leading the group is always going to be a priority for him. He will spend a lot of his time and effort in his alpha arena. Whether it is work or sports or organizations, the alpha male needs a place where he is the leader. If you expect to be the only focus of his attention, you will have a hard time in this relationship.

An alpha will put a lot of pressure to succeed on you and on his children.

Other women will pursue an alpha even if he is married.

If You Want an Alpha Male

If you still want an alpha male, you must be an alpha female in his arena. Look around at the women who are pursued as partners by the men in that arena. Notice the qualities these men are seeking. In addition to such details as clothes, manners, and so on, there are some basic attributes of the alpha female:

She is a leader of the other females. This does not mean using power the way men do but using her female sensitivity to bond with the other women in the group in a way that makes them look up to her.

She is physically attractive in a way that conforms to the group's ideal.

She exudes a certain class and style that sets her apart from the others in a dignified way.

She is smart, both intellectually and emotionally.

She is often a caretaker for the group's females and offspring. She takes responsibility.

———

Nicholas was raised on speed. He skied fast, raced cars and motorcycles, anything that went fast. He lived in the world of men who sought speed. A regular Johnathan Livingston Seagull, but Nicholas wanted speed on Earth terms, so there was gravity to deal with and injuries.

When he walked into a room, even when no one knew his history, men bowed their heads in acknowledgment of an alpha. Women loved him.

When he began dating Sarah, she adored him but realized that she was in a unique situation. Sarah was a counselor and she had her own milieu, one quite different from the world Nicholas inhabited.

His priorities were not in relationships but motion. He was really very sweet in their relationship, but if an opportunity came up to race, he just got caught up in it and disappeared.

When he was with her, he was wonderful—loving, intense, and, most of all, present. When he was away, he didn't call, he didn't make dates except at the spur of the moment, and for all she knew he never gave her a second thought.

Sarah was busy enough with her own life that it didn't bother her much at first. He came and went and she just made room for him.

After a while, he began to take her to the races with him. She felt honored. Sarah was a Bordeaux type of woman, but she cheerfully spent the day in the pits drinking beer and eating whatever dusty food was available.

She liked seeing Nicholas on his own turf. He pretty much left her on her own as he talked to the other racers. He especially liked helping young people who were just beginning and needed the advice of an old pro. Sarah enjoyed these days. It was interesting to watch him in his own realm. It was a bit frightening for Sarah to see him race—there was danger everywhere, and at high speed—but it was exhilarating, too. Sarah felt honored to bask in his reflected honor in this place where he was clearly respected.

It was fairly easy for Sarah to live the relationship this way during the summer, but with fall came a load of counseling work of her own.

Nicholas had no interest in modifying his life in any way to make room for her needs. They tried to keep things going, but gradually the pressures of their separate lives took their toll.

They drifted apart without much stress. It didn't occur to Sarah to try to change him, and she didn't feel that she wanted to live her life as a racing groupie.

She also knew that there were always plenty of young women around him. Without her presence he would just find one who was more flexible and live his life his own way.

And so he did.

———

Most People Don't Need to Be Alpha

You can eliminate a lot of stress and self-esteem problems if you simply decide that you don't need to be an alpha female. Indeed, most women don't. They're happier fitting comfortably into an ordinary life. They like their men to come home and spend time with the family. Most people are just happier this way.

But it's hard to avoid feeling that you haven't lived up to your potential if you haven't succeeded in becoming alpha. This is expressed by the words, "I could have done better."

If what you want, however, is a home and family and vacations that don't include the whole pack or the pack's activities, then you would not be happy with an alpha.

You need to look around at the wider selection that is all around you. Find the nice, noncompetitive guys who just work hard and love who they love. These men do not expect you to be a perfect reflection of their ambitions. They like who you are. They really enjoy leaving the rat race at the end of the day and coming home.

Most women are happiest with these men. But the same women seem to think that they need to prove themselves by pursuing an alpha. If you are in this group, you may want to rethink this goal. The search for alpha status is not everything you need to know about relationships, but it is a seldom-discussed area that you should consider if you are looking for reasons why your choices are not working.

Two alphas are likely to be together to accomplish something. People of other ranks are more likely to be the kind of soul mates who put their relationship first. Both are legitimate soul mates, but it is important to know the difference. If you are looking for a close, comfortable soul mate, despite your biological inclinations toward rising in the hierarchy, you might not find what you want with an alpha.

Another Category

There is another group, smaller but interesting. These are the people—male or female—who are simply independent. Most of the time they don't often work in groups, but they can take over as alpha if it is needed. They won't settle into the role very often, though; they just do it for a while and then go on their way.

They tend to choose their mates because they like them the way they are. They do not force their lives into any molds. You would need to be pretty flexible to choose a mate like this, but it would always be interesting.

They don't settle down very often into a routine, or if they do they don't stay for long. If you are looking for stability and security, stay away from these wanderers.

You can have a nice relationship with an independent, though, if you are one yourself. If you love a new challenge and have a lot going on in your own life, this might be a perfect choice for you. If you don't expect a life that is completely shared, or completely predictable, this could be your mate. Or if you are looking for someone to just kick around with who will give you room to have your own life, this kind of person might be just right for you.

What you don't want to do is to find one of these independent people and then try to change him. It won't work and you will feel rejected.

Some Things Men Should Remember About Women

A man has only one escape from his old self: to see a differ-
ent self in the mirror of some woman's eyes.

—Clare Boothe Luce

The lessons of the alpha apply to women, too. It is important for men to know that with women, the alpha competition is very sub-liminal. Women will rather happily find a mate who is not com-peting for alpha status and not give it another thought. This is because men are masters of power and very aware of that quali-ty, but women are masters of emotion. Once emotion is the issue, competition is irrelevant to women.

Because men's power issues are pretty straightforward, women's emotional issues may seem very convoluted to men. The underlying condition that define the instinctive level of women's emotional motivation has everything to do with the fact that nature made them to be mothers.

Their motivations, at least at the beginning of their desire for a relationship, are:

To find a mate who will be the best parent, both genetically and practically.

To create a relationship supportive enough to make a safe place for her children.

That sounds simple until you add a couple of social changes that complicate the issue. For the last several thousand years, a woman has taken her status from the man to whom she is attached—and this remains pretty solidly in place. So a woman will try to find the man with the highest status available, but he is not always her wisest choice, because high-status males spend a lot of their time holding on to that status and trying to reach the next level. This does not make them the ideal family nurturers. But it is highly ingrained socially.

Add to this the fact that over the last twenty or thirty years women have begun to feel that they too must have their own accomplishment in a career to be considered successful.

This second condition does not preclude the first; it adds to it, and often works at cross-purposes. This is one reason why women are confusing.

Men's lives are much more straightforward than women's lives.

Women, because their lives are about nurturing, are encouraged from the time they are little girls to be emotionally aware. They express their emotions, they often feel other people's feelings just like they were their own, and they place value on emotional realities.

Men, whose lives are essentially competitive, are taught from childhood to put emotions aside and concentrate on the task at hand. This does not mean that men don't have emotions, because of course they do. But their emotional knowledge is not usually developed; they are not generally as good at expressing emotions as women are. For this reason men are not as comfortable dealing with emotional interactions as women feel necessary to the bonding process.

The Biological Clock

There often comes a time in a childless woman's life when she experiences something called the ticking of the biological clock. It's more intense than it sounds—the physical and emotional cravings for a child can be completely overwhelming.

If you are around her at this time of her life, which can happen anywhere from ages twenty-one to thirty-five—or older, if she has no children—then you are being considered as the father of her children. You are not just her lover, not just a romantic liaison, but a potential coparent. It may not be what you are looking for in the relationship, but it is certainly what she needs.

But there's more to the picture. Because a woman has certain timing and biological imperatives, she seeks different kinds of men at different times of her life. The man she might form a family with at twenty is likely not the companion and playmate she will seek in her forties.

There are three distinct stages of a woman's adulthood, each marked by a physiological change. The maiden part of life begins with the onset of menses. The term *maiden* has nothing to do with sexual experience or the lack of it; it refers to the time of young adulthood and courtship. The next phase, the mother, begins with bearing a child. The crone or elder phase begins with menopause.

Each of these phases is determined by the one thing about women that men often forget when considering a relationship:

A woman is physically the vessel of life.

You might not want to deal with this fact if you are a man looking for a soul mate, but a great deal of why women behave can be traced to it. This also applies to women who choose not to have children or to have more children. Even menopause is intimately related to this childbearing reality.

Women may deny it, men may want to ignore it, employers may pretend it is not there, but women are women because of this one thing. Or we wouldn't have a human race.

Perhaps it is because we are trying to ignore this as a society that the female ideal these days is a thin, slim-hipped, small-breasted woman. But if you look at pictures from any other time, you will notice the ideal looks like a woman in her childbearing years. In fact, she has the very figure that many women today are fighting to lose. Full breasts, round hips, and a round belly define the shape of a healthy adult female. A woman is not obese just because she is shaped like a woman.

Even if you have found a career woman who is absolutely not interested in having a family, these physical facts will remain true. She will still have monthly cycles; her body will still change shape according to the timing of her fertility. And hormones, which are a part of her reproductive system, rule her sex drive.

This should be very basic information, but men tend to forget this side of a woman's life unless they are actively trying to make a baby. It is a reality for women, whether it is convenient or not.

Now these hormones aren't any more mysterious and compelling than, say, testosterone. It is just that they operate toward a different end. And their phases are more predictable and subtle.

By the way, an interesting phenomenon occurs when women spend a lot of their time in a group like an office: They synchronize their cycles. It means that their ups and downs are magnified. So it is a good idea to know that women's cycles are not all about moodiness. There are times of glorious ups and sexiness and outward energy at the beginning of the cycle. The second half of the cycle is about pulling inward; you will see slight irritations if she is interrupted from this inner dynamic. The things that bother women now should be taken seriously; they're things she ignored during the beginning of her cycle and can no longer. You will find that during the second half of their cycles, women are more like men. They are much less inclined to bury important issues because they want to be compliant. They speak up and even become quite assertive and competitive at this time. During their menses, women often enjoy being in the company of other women, or else just being alone. It is a very inward time. Emotions and nerves might be a little more on edge.

We have been taught that the moon lodge—a structure to which women once withdrew during their menses—was used because men wanted them to be separated from the group. We later learned that during that time it is far easier to be in the company of women. No doubt, it was the women who chose this method of withdrawal from responsibilities. The expectation that you will be pleasant when you wish to be grumpy does not exist in the women's lodge. Grumpy is allowed and there is no man getting irritated about it.

Here is a nice tip: Often when a group of women has their cycles coordinated, they follow a regular moon cycle: The new moon marks the beginning of their cycle with midcycle or ovulation occurring at the full moon. Once you get used to this you can easily tell what to expect by simply looking up.

But women's emotions come from far more than their hormones. Women are often taught that they are responsible for the emotions in the people around them. They have a second nature about these things that they developed by their own natural emotional awareness and the teachings they received as children. Even those women who don't really enjoy emotional experiences have usually learned to use emotions in interesting ways in their lives and those of the people close to them.

Nurturing is a part of the woman's natural role. Nurturing is a very emotional business. It includes the need to deal with the testosterone leading the other camp—to heal the emotions of people who have been enveloped all day in the testosterone and adrenaline of competition. Such emotional healing is needed almost daily.

It works out rather nicely that women deal well with emotions.

These days, when a women may spend all day in the competitive arena—and remember, she has lots of adrenaline and a fair amount of testosterone, too—she may feel it would be nice to go home to some nurturing, too. That is often why she wants to talk when she gets home, while you are dealing with the whole thing by wanting to be quiet.

The Dance—Beginning to Connect

Do you want to know a good way to fall in love? Just associate with all your pleasant experiences with someone, and disassociate from all the unpleasant ones.

—Richard Bandler

Ah, falling in love, It makes you happy, it makes you crazy, it pushes all of your alive buttons. It is wonderful and terrifying.

When you find a soul mate and fall in love, the dance gets

faster. It is often love at first sight. And even though you are sec-ond-guessing yourself all the way, you know that this is going to be something important.

One of the first things you notice is that the soul mate doesn't seem like he or she is made of the same materials as other people. There is something more electric, more alive, and more com-pelling about this person the first time you find yourself in his or her presence.

You may find yourself asking people, "Who *is* that?" over and over. You may ask yourself the same thing. Even after you finally meet and when it is supposed to be apparent who this is (in con-ventional terms).

Things can move very quickly when you meet a soul mate. This may not seem wise at the time, but you need to really follow your instincts. And of course, the soul-mate experience needs to be sep-arated from the normal attractions that are governed by your sex-ual drive—a formidable force of its own. The feeling is different, though, even when it includes a fair amount of sexual tension and the soul mate who has appeared in your life to be your lover.

Some very obvious things happen when men and women begin to become attracted to one another. The meeting itself is usually more intense. This can be a bit scary. Because soul mates often dance a little faster.

––––––

It was a party. Amanda was happily perched right in the middle of things. On the far side of the little group she noticed Ben, a writer friend. He was talking to someone she had never seen before.

There were several odd things about this. Even though they were talking quite quietly, Amanda could hear every word they said. She was carrying on conversations with her friends, as well as hearing the whole conversation of the men.

It was about the finer points of motorcycles and she found it fascinating. This was an oddity in itself, because even though she had had a motorcycle years ago and loved it, she had virtually no interest in how it worked or how to make it do anything at all bet-ter than what it just did.

Amanda couldn't take her eyes off this new man. He was a bit craggy with a gray beard and a very unassuming manner. He was dressed in the everyman style: jeans, a plain shirt, a leather bomber jacket. Nothing terribly noticeable about him except that he was compelling her interest yet he had no idea that she was there at all.

She tried to focus back on the people she was with. She talked to them and listened to them and still heard every word the man was saying.

Soon she began to convince herself that they had a lot of things in common. Since she had limited knowledge of motorcycle parts, Amanda couldn't quite say what those things might be.

So as she left she stopped by to see Ben, said hello, said good night, was introduced to Casey, and promptly handed him her business card, brazenly telling him, "You need to call me." She walked out.

Amanda didn't hear from Casey, which didn't really surprise her. But they had overlapping circles of friends. She would be at a party or get-together and suddenly feel something at the back of her neck like a tingle. She'd turn around and he would be there...usually across the room and not seeing her, but there.

When he was anywhere near her, she couldn't take her eyes off him. She was still seeing someone else but Casey just drew her attention.

Things slowly changed. She and her boyfriend broke up, the encounters with Casey became more regular, and he slowly moved closer, though it took a couple of months. Finally, one night, they had a very careful conversation. It happened like this:

Amanda wandered into the club after a party that was ghastly. She needed to see people she actually liked. It was Friday, the place was crowded, but she found a seat at the bar with her friends.

She settled in. She was not feeling social.

The words, "Can you pass me my drink?" came from behind her. A finger pointed at a tall glass on the bar.

She picked up the drink and turned to pass it to the voice. "Here you go," she said and noticed it was Casey.

"Thanks," he said politely and turned to rejoin his friends, who were ensconced against the wall behind her.

She resumed her chat with her own friends and almost forgot Casey was behind her.

Then he bumped into her as someone was trying to pass and excused himself. She smiled. Her attention returned to her friends. She wasn't feeling like flirting, she just wanted comfortable talk with people she liked.

She felt a little pressure on her back. "Uh, those two?" said the voice. She knew who it was and followed the pointing finger to another glass of the same and a beer; she turned to pass them on. This time she was relaxing a bit and gave him a small smile. To which he responded, "Do you have a light?" and held up a cigarette.

She handed him a lighter, still turned toward him. He lit his cigarette, looked at her for a minute, and said, "Thanks." Then he returned back to his friends.

Damn, Amanda thought, I need to get this right out of my head. I'm just being a waitress here. And again she turned to talk to her little group. She was a bit mad at herself for flirting with him after all this time only to be dismissed again.

A slight pressure from the right and she saw him leaning against the bar, still focused on his friends but, because the place was getting more crowded, very much into her space.

Soon he turned around to order another drink and asked for still another light. She handed him the lighter and pulled out her own cigarette, which he lit. Of course, he had to. "That's the longest cigarette I ever saw," he observed.

"It's a girl cigarette. See," she said, holding it up, "it has flowers."

"Can I try one?" he asked.

Now this was interesting. Most men wouldn't do this. Most men are very threatened by girl things, Amanda knew, as if they'd fill them up with estrogen and emasculate them or something. This man obviously liked women and was very confident about his own masculinity.

She liked that. He bought her a drink.

She was prepared to begin to get to know him now. He smiled and turned back to his friends. Maybe, she thought, I should just go. As she was considering that, she heard his voice again. "This cigarette tastes good," he said. She noticed her friends had vacated the next barstool. He moved over to it.

He told her he had just gotten back from Daytona for some national motorcycle races. And that he raced dirt bikes in the summer. "Even though I'm kind of an old man for that," he added sheepishly.

He was turning out to be not at all what she expected. He was quite accomplished in a man's-man way. He had lived a great deal of his life in the world of sports. Not conventional, professional sports, but impressive. But he related all of this in a mild and self-effacing manner that was downright sweet. Who was this guy?

After excusing herself to find a rest room, Amanda returned to find both of their seats occupied. He was talking to a women she didn't know. She got her coat and said good night as she walked by.

"You're going?" he asked. He actually sounded disappointed.

"Things to do tomorrow," she more or less lied. With a wave, she was gone.

———

With a soul mate you will often find unexpected parallels in your lives. You will find something more than just normal attraction. Soul mates compel each other even in the first minutes. If their fear of the intensity pushes them away, something else, something they can't name, draws them back.

———

Thursday evening Amanda went to a visualization meeting at Unity church. On the way home, she wanted some company and stopped off at the club to see who would be around. As she entered she noticed there were two separate groups of friends there, both glad to see her. It was just what she needed that night—some companionship and good talk.

On the far right was a group of creative people she had worked with off and on for years. In the corner on the left were the professors from the university, who were always good for conversation.

In the middle there was someone in a trench coat with its back to her. She went to her right first, and joined the conversation. From there she could see that Casey was in the big trench coat. Facing the bar, he didn't notice her at all. She walked past him to talk to the professors and get a drink.

After they chatted for a while she returned to the creative group. She was interested to hear if there was anything going on in the arts community that might result in a job.

Soon she wandered toward the professors' corner, but an arm appeared out of the trench coat and pulled her toward the bar. Casey said, "Sit down."

Interesting approach, she thought, direct, I like it.

After a bit of small talk, he looked at her and said, "I used to be a knight in England, around thirteen, fourteen hundred."

Well, *that* got her attention. She wanted to be careful not to spook him. If she told him she had been having past-life regressions to that same time and place since she returned from a trip to England, she was sure he would not be able to handle it. She really didn't want him to run away.

"No kidding," she replied carefully. "Maybe I knew you. I was there, too."

He quickly began to backpedal. "I don't know if I believe in that stuff."

She knew he was going to do that. "Well, I know I do," she said. "I've had too many confirmations to doubt it, but you can believe what you want."

He began to tell her how natural he was the first time he had been around horses a few years ago. How he'd won a rodeo after only two weeks of riding. "It was like I had done it before."

They spoke of Europe and a mutual love of England. She had been to the Caribbean the year before and he told her about taking a year off work and sailing around there. They talked for hours, like old friends.

She mentioned giving him her business card several months before. He said he didn't remember it at all. He held her hand while they were talking at the end of the evening, then walked her to her car. They said good night.

———

Of course, they saw each other again and finally began a lovely relationship. Remember: Soul-mate relationships are meant to be. You can relax. If this is a soul mate, you will get together. Even if it seems impossible or takes years to really begin, it will happen if the beginning felt right. There is no need to let them make you crazy.

Keeping It Working—The Beginning

Each friend represents a world in us, a world not born until they arrive, and it is only by this meeting that a new world is born.

—Anaïs Nin

As you begin a relationship with your soul mate, the first thing you want to do is to let the relationship be what it is. Spirit has put this person in your life right now because there are gifts in it for you both. Give yourself permission to enjoy this beginning time— to celebrate one of the wonder of your life. Give this beginning all the time and attention that it deserves.

Forget everything that happened to you in relationships before this. Let go of the past. You have done all your forgiveness and release work, so you needn't expect that this relationship will repeat the past. This is the not time to let little worries and fears and frustrations that are old patterns from your past interfere.

Your new soul mate comes to your life full of potential and promise. Honor that. You are just where you should be. Let it unfold.

Don't be afraid to be romantic. This is the time when you should do the flowers and the dinners in dimly lit places. Dress nicely. Indulge yourself, let the moon be magical again. A long walk, holding hands, can set your heart soaring.

Enjoy being part of your own romance. This is the time for the two of you to find all the common ground you share. It is a time to explore potentials. If your knees are weak and your head is spinning, this is as it should be. Spirit is bonding you in her most delightful dance. Be conscious in the moment as you star in your own romantic movie.

Try not to rush things. It won't be easy. The tendency with soul mates is to hurry into sexual bonding. But try to linger a while with your kisses; enjoy the little thrill as your hands touch.

Like a dance, the man should think he is leading. Relationships are best when the man gets a chance to win the woman and the woman feels that he has worked a bit to win her. It is the way our social order has been for a long time. It makes both people feel valued, so it is important. Because men and women are equal does not mean they are the same. We have different needs. It is all part of the dance.

Stay positive. Don't look for problems that aren't there. Don't worry that it is too good to be true. Worry may be the most useless thing we ever do, but to spoil this wonderful time with it is to dishonor your love and yourself. You don't want to fall into that trap. Don't obsess about your partner's last affiliation. Don't obsess about anything. You can now begin to let go of obsessive tendencies, because you don't need them anymore.

Dream beautiful dreams and get out of the way of letting them come true.

Talk to positive people. When you are not together with your soul mate, spend your time with the friends who honestly wish you well. This is no time to be talking to people who find fault with everything. You are creating your dreams now, you don't want to create negative outcomes.

Toxic people are especially taxing at any time, they can cause a lot of undue stress and misunderstandings. They have no business influencing you at this time. If this means you have to keep your distance from some family members, that is okay. If you just can't do that, try not to talk to them about your new interest until you are more sure of it.

This is your time. You make the choices. You can cast your movie as well as star in it. Don't let anyone rain on your parade!

Pay attention to your own feelings and the directions you get from your heart. Banish the worries and fears; they have no place here.

Beyond the Beginning—The Transition After the First Month

Life is a series of collisions with the future; it is not the sum of what we have been, but what we yearn to be.

—José Ortega y Gasset

Falling in love is the glue that bonds the two of you, but as you move beyond that (usually at three to six weeks), you need to take each other into your real lives.

Here you will find the real story of whether it will work for any length of time or not.

A little preparation will help, as will the positive knowledge that if your soul mate cares for you, he or she will probably be comfortable with the life that formed you.

In fact, you will often find that since the people in your family are definitely your soul mates, and this new love is a soul mate, they might have a few lives in common themselves.

There will be a lot of give and take here. The older you are, the more will be required. This is because you are pretty well psychologically formed and not likely to be able to make major life changes for someone else. However, the older you are, the more patience and experience you have; you can take time to work things out.

It is a good thing to be as honest as possible about the way you really operate and the things that really bother you. You might be convinced when you are starting that the annoying little things your partner does just don't bother you. You may even find them endearing. But as you go on, these same things might get under your skin enough to harm the relationship. So tell your partner what you really don't like and see what you can do about starting the habits from the beginning that will help the relationship in the long run. There is also more of a spirit of cooperation at the beginning when the bonds between you are growing.

This time of adjustment is best taken slowly. The bonding that you do at the beginning of a relationship will go a long way later on toward establishing the patterns you need in someone you can live with.

The younger you are, the more natural this adjustment period is, because you are still forming. It is much simpler for both of you to take on the patterns of another person. But do not deny who you really are because you think your lover wants something else. If you are in a relationship that will last, your partner needs to love you for exactly who you are. This is not possible if you are not being yourself.

One of the hardest things we can do in a relationship is to expose our true selves, especially the parts for which we have been criticized in the past. In intimate relationships, political correctness goes only so far.

For instance, if your partner is going to be dealing with your temper in the relationship, don't try to pretend that you are always on an even keel. Some people need a good fight now and then to get to intimacy. Not cheap shots or cruelty, but yelling and disagreements will happen. Don't pretend they won't.

If your emotional outlet tends toward sarcasm, it is best to see how your partner deals with this as soon as possible. Some people really glory in this; they enjoy a good verbal sparring complete with sarcasm, bons mots, and double entendres. Some people find this tedious and prefer a good yell. It is best to know who you are dealing with.

If you have any variances in temperament, they must be addressed. You can learn to deal with another style of argument, but only if you know what it is going to be.

Of course the very best thing is to find someone who has roughly the same style as you do. So you may want to add that quality to your list.

Some issues come up often. Smokers date nonsmokers; drinkers (not alcoholics, just drinkers) can get involved with nondrinkers; morning people get involved with night people. Often the nonsmoker, nondrinker, or early riser will be inclined to put a moral label on these qualities. That is a bad idea. If you intend to continue the relationship, it will be counterproductive.

If you really cannot tolerate these habits, do not get involved with these people.

Probably you were interested in them in the first place because they were unique, nonconformist, and a bit adventurous and interesting. They know that in the modern world, these habits are politically incorrect. They have taken that issue and most others into consideration and chosen what they will do.

Attempts to criticize or shame or coerce them will not be effective. In fact, since they tend to be nonconformists, such efforts will likely trigger the opposite reaction. If they are ready to quit, they'll quit; if they decide they want to get up in the morning, they'll get up. (This doesn't mean that they will fall asleep easily at your appointed time, by the way. Sleep patterns can be dictated by body clocks, or a need for silence in which to be creative, or any number of life conditions.)

If you are the smoker, drinker, or night person in a relationship, you will have to decide how to cope with the pressures to change. Or you will have to resign yourself to a lot of arguments—or ending the relationship.

If you eat only Chinese food and your partner likes French and northern Italian, well, that has no real moral weight. You will have to experiment and learn to deal with it. Or your mate might have very refined taste in decor, while you like life a bit more crude or unsophisticated. All these things will need compromise. The areas you will find most difficult are those where one partner makes a moral judgment about the other's habits.

If you feel strongly about any of the issues in this section, go back to your list and change it!

It is very necessary in a relationship to accept the other for exactly what he or she is. Even if that's not exactly like you. These days, when people can be so judgmental, it is even more important. You need this kind of love and acceptance, and so does your partner.

The Shadow Side

We all have a shadow side. It is that part of us that is just never politically correct. Some of us hide it very well. Some of us are completely unaware of its existence. Most are in denial of at least some part of their shadow.

You know it. You can hear it, those little voices in your head that you know will be "unacceptable" if spoken aloud. Often they are fun, but you don't want to admit it. You would hate hearing these things from someone else.

Everyone has this. It is ultimately the part of you that gives you form.

Pure light is lovely. But pure light has no form. It is only light's interplay with shadow that lets us see something solid.

In a relationship this is a double-edged sword because both partners have shadow sides. And in the beginning, both are hiding them carefully. We present our best, our most acceptable sides as we are getting to know someone. This is normal.

The first feelings of connection, therefore, involve the other person in an incomplete way. And you, yourself, are not perceived completely, either. You may feel that things are shaky because you have an unconscious awareness that your partner doesn't know you.

This takes time. You have to learn to trust this person, and vice versa, before either of you can see the other completely; before you can allow each other even a glimpse of the shadow side.

Sometimes the shadow side of the other is a pure delight. A sharp-edged way of seeing things or a wicked sense of humor is often stored in the shadow. But other times it is a very difficult thing to live with—involving a lifetime of resentment or control.

This is the reason that you can't always tell at the beginning if a relationship will work. You just don't have a clear picture of the whole person until you see the hidden side.

Once you have seen it, it is entirely possible that it will be a thing that you can live with without much difficulty. It is also possible that you cannot. But you must experience it if you are to judge.

In the best relationships, the shadow side becomes a mutual secret form of delight. You really appreciate the edge that it gives to the partnership, and your partner finds that your little dark side is a bit of spice. Relationships like this can go on for a good long time. There is far less judgment and more intimacy in this sort of acceptance.

So take your time. Don't make big commitments until you are sure that you know the whole person, not just the person being presented as lovable. You may find a trickster there or you may find a source of fascination, but wait to see what it really is before you make any real commitment.

A Little Bit About Sexuality

First, your sexual body is your reproductive body. This is an easy thing to forget when you are in love. Making a baby is a beautiful thing to do. But it is not the purpose of the sort of sex that you have at the beginning of a relationship. That time is to promote intimacy.

Having sex is a natural thing to do. However, having sex that expands and extends your intimacy in a way that is satisfying to both partners requires some patience and sensitivity. Still, don't take it so seriously that you are not having fun.

An overview of sexuality requires an age-group survey again.

Very young, sexually mature men and women have essentially different sex drives. Young men (under twenty-one) are driven by sex to an extent that a woman of the same age can't even begin to understand.

Young men are having sexual thoughts most of the time. The fact that they can control them is remarkable. Women at this age are much more romantic, seeking love and the little gestures that go along with it. This can and often does lead to sex, but sex is not the driving force for the woman involved.

In her twenties, a woman's sex drive might lag, but it comes back strong in her thirties. By his own thirties a man has mellowed out a bit and is often caught by surprise at the ardor of his partner.

And so it goes. It is always an adventure, because things change. It can be a frustration. But remember that no one is perfect at sex, and no one's even good at it until they have experience. And the learning can be a lot of fun.

It is crucial to communicate when it comes to sex. But there is such sensitivity around the subject that this can be difficult. This is no reason to stop trying.

Sex, like other parts of the relationship, requires that the people involved love themselves enough to feel comfortable with intimacy. If you are going to get naked with this person, you had better find a way to get comfortable with it.

If you're in your teens, it is common, as you watch your body changing, to be a little put off by the process and want to hide it under clothes. But at some point, it is a good idea to get comfortable with your own skin.

It is also important to know that sex is about loving each other—a physical way to honor your love for each other. You don't want just a quick, groping roll in the hay; that will leave both partners feeling dissatisfied and disillusioned. Still, whatever is comfortable to you is okay.

Good sex, then, is a very important part of a relationship. It helps to be very knowledgeable about the subject. The information you get from friends about sexuality is not reliable. Schools teach only the biology of sex, not sexuality, and are not much help.

Your parents have probably shied away from giving you the real information that you need. And even adult friends who are not your parents are reluctant to talk to you about it lest they interfere with your parents' attitudes.

But there is information available. There are many books about various aspects of sexuality. If you have a question, the information is there. Don't be afraid to read the adult books. Just stay away from the porn; it doesn't teach much of anything. Take the time to learn the essentials.

Then talk to each other about it. Find out what each of you needs or wants.

Even if you're older, sex is a subject that you will never stop wanting to learn about. Even when you are quite experienced—almost especially then—you can learn more interesting things. The same depth that you find in emotion you can find in sex, because sex is wrapped in emotion.

The most common mistake that people make about sex is thinking they know all about it. Every partner is an adventure and everyone is different.

For example: A man has learned that women need foreplay. So he gets really good at foreplay; in fact, that's what most of sex becomes for him. The actual sex act might just last a few minutes. Lots of women like this.

Then he meets a woman who like a little foreplay but prefers the sex act itself to go on for a lot longer. This is what he always thought he really wanted, but old habits are hard to break. Once he's done so, he is happy about it. Then the next woman he meets wants something quite different.

It is important to know your own body and needs, and it important to know what your partner needs, too. You can be sure that those two things will be different, but complementary.

It is also important to honor your own sexuality and that of your partner by remaining present, conscious, open to see what is best at any given time. Sex is communication. You will not have satisfying sex if you switch to automatic pilot when you are participating in it.

Take the time to honor your sexuality with knowledge and openness to new ideas.

═══════

BODY-AWARENESS TIPS FOR WOMEN

Many young women feel that they are not attractive enough because they don't look like the people whom they consider ideal—models. The truth is that no one expects you to be a model; a man who cares for you usually likes you just the way you are. You are already perfectly desirable to your partner. Do not be self-conscious because you do not feel perfect.

Furthermore, neither you nor anyone you know will ever look like the models in the magazines. Why? Because those women don't look like that either. Despite being taller and slimmer than normal women, their images are computer enhanced in the photos.

In the presence of a really successful model, you would want to feed her. She is so thin that she looks like she just left a concentration camp. The camera puts ten pounds on her but the computer retouching takes it off again. In person, this is not a good look.

Lately the fashion has been what they call "heroin-chic"— the look of a person who is emaciated because of a drug habit. That is, needless to say, something you do not want to emulate.

A few other things you should know about models. Their job is not to look good, but to make the clothes look good. There is something alarming about a grown woman trying to starve herself to look like a fourteen-year-old boy.

Women are women shaped. It is often helpful to look at pictures of women from years past (before 1960): You will see things like breasts, hips, and bellies. Women are shaped that way and it is beautiful.

The average woman is five foot four and 140 pounds. It has been that way for years. This does not match the present ideal, but it is a physical reality. It is about the size of the women the French Impressionists painted, beautiful soft nudes. It is the size of classical representations of the goddesses. These were not tiny, boy-shaped women.

Be proud of who you are.

A woman's body changes during the course of her life. This is because it is adjusting in various ways to her relationship to reproduction. It will often grow bigger here and smaller there according to the dictates of estrogen, and other hormones.

Some women can eat anything they want until they are in their early twenties; and then they find that they put on quite a lot of weight very easily. Some women have a baby and slim right down again; some hold on to extra weight for years. Lots of women slim down in their thirties only to turn forty and have their bellies pop out no matter what they do.

In a world with only one image of beauty this can be disconcerting. But look around. It is not only perfect-looking people who have relationships. As a matter of fact, men often like women who are shaped exactly like women.

So look at the mirror when you are naked and find those things that you like about being woman shaped. Consider your body as it is itself; don't expect it to fit someone else's ideal. You should be the one who knows that you are beautiful. That knowledge spins a glamour around you that other people will see.

You can and should get a new haircut now and then, use makeup to enhance your features, and dress nicely, but it is the strut of confidence that tells the people around you that you are beautiful. And that strut comes from loving yourself.

Remember that it is you with whom your partner has chosen to be involved. There is no need to be self-conscious because you don't look like those models in the magazines. He probably wouldn't like them anyway.

━━━━

BODY-AWARENESS TIPS FOR MEN

Men are often less self-critical about looks than women, but they do have concerns about their attractiveness. Men are very visually oriented in their sexuality. They fall in lust with their eyes. They often expect women to be the same way. Women, however, tend to fall in love with something more than the physical. A man's voice, gestures, words are very important to women. The courtship ritual is a form of honoring a woman. A man who understands that is apt to be very attractive.

Younger women are looking for a man who will be able to take care of them and their children. They rarely realize it at the time, but the qualities that really appeal to them are often linked to this need. This is where men first get the idea that women want guys with money. What she really wants is a man who will provide security for herself and her children.

Especially for younger men: Reread "Most People Don't Need to Be Alpha" on page 87. Many women feel that if they are good enough, they will win an alpha male. These days, though, alpha men do not make the best partners for most women.

Men, too, look for women at the top levels of attractiveness to prove their own alpha qualities. Again, these women are not often your best choice for a partner.

What *is* important is letting your partner know that she is attractive to you, and taking the time she needs to work up to a sexual experience. This is especially true after you have been together for a while. Body awareness for a man has less to do with his own attractiveness than is does with being aware of the body next to him.

As a man gets older, however, he can get too comfortable with himself. He may feel that even when he's out of shape, a woman will see the same old handsome kid he always was. This is not necessarily the case. He needs to pay attention. Healthy and clean are important. Neatness counts, too. It is easy to slip into a rut; remember, though, that as you get older it takes more effort to look as attractive as it was natural to look when you were younger. Styles change; take a look at your clothes and your hair and see if you are keeping up. Women do notice.

The male sexual drive is usually pretty straightforward. Women operate on a different clock.

When a relationship becomes sexual, it is very important to

be very aware of who it is you are with. Do not take for granted that she will be the same as other partners. Get to know her
specifically and sexually.

It is very important to a woman that you want to have sex
with her because she is very attractive to you. It is not important to her that you just want to do it now. *This does not change
as you get farther into the relationship.*

Very often the sexiest thing you can do as far as a woman is
concerned is to refrain from going into automatic pilot in the
bedroom. Focus instead on being consciously present with
your partner during sex.

========

Other People—Blending Family, Friends, and Work Relationships

*Were we to love none who had imperfections, this would be
a desert for our love. All we can do is to make the best of our
friends; love and cherish what is good in them, and keep out
of the way of what is bad: but no more think of rejecting
them for it than of throwing away a piece of music for a flat
passage or two.*

—Thomas Jefferson

Because people tend to reincarnate in groups with quite a history,
it is fairly likely that when you find your soul mate, you will also
find that other people in your life have some issues with him or her.

These may make it easier and more natural to integrate your
partner into your life. But things can also go the other way: You
can run across old negative issues that need to be resolved. Family
is the likeliest place for this to happen, but if your friends feel that
you have known them for a couple of lifetimes, they may be
involved, too. You will see this almost immediately—these people
will take an instant like or dislike to your partner.

This is all part of the plan and underscores that what you have
found is not just another relationship but a real soul mate.

You can't completely eliminate that this is an issue from this life, though. If there is jealousy, or if one of your friends has a way of coming on to every partner you have, you can't count this friend as a soul mate of your partner.

It is wise to keep your individual friendships while you continue to introduce your new partner into them. There is a difference in the dynamic between two women friends and one friend and a pair. The whole rhythm of the thing changes; you will lose some of the intimacy of a friendship that took you years to create.

So certainly keep introducing your partner into activities, but stay in touch with your friends and their concerns, too. Meet them for lunch or play now and again alone.

Here's a tip: Take one evening a week and use it to keep your friends close individually. As lovely as it is to have a new relationship, these people have been with you for years and you need to value the individuality of each friendship.

Work situations are usually easier. Indeed, when social functions are involved everybody will be more comfortable if you are part of a couple. The rest of your work life isn't that social anyway, so it shouldn't be a big deal. Unless you work in a very small, intimate company, you will probably not be dealing much with karma at work.

Then there is the family dynamic. No doubt you have learned to live with a certain amount of dysfunction and a crazy relative or two whom you know is harmless, but when you think of introducing your shiny new lover to them all it seems appalling.

Even the best families will trot out the embarrassing history or share the pictures of you in the 1970s with outrageous hair and huge bell-bottoms or love beads. This is all normal stuff, and eventually you'll have to meet your partner's family, too, along with its uncle lecher or cousin conspiracy-fanatic. Relax and just try to deal with the moments.

It is kind, though, to let your partner know if there are any unusual situations in your family. If you have an uncle who sits in a corner and hallucinates as a lifestyle, but you dearly love him, let your partner know what is going on. If Dad drinks too much and gets out of line, or Sister can be expected to hit on your new beau, or Uncle will hug the new girlfriend a little too long, you know it is pretty normal, but your partner doesn't. So prepare him or her for this encounter to avoid embarrassment for anybody.

More difficult is the family that you have created—your children. Of all your significant others, these are the only ones whose needs must come before those of your relationship.

It is best, at first, to introduce them slowly to your new love. Have your time together when the children are somewhere else, if possible. Children, especially little children, can become attached very quickly to a nice person whom a parent loves. They need to be protected a bit from forming too close an emotional tie when it is not clear what kind of relationship this is going to be.

Children need more emotional stability as they learn what a loving relationship is about. It is not good for them to get close to one partner after another who seems to care for them and then leaves. This can raise abandonment issues.

So keep a bit of an emotional distance with the kids until you are sure that this relationship will be a real part of your life. And then expect some kind of assurance from your partner that the children will be considered in future issues between the two of you.

Restructuring—Changes That Keep It Going

Love is not only something you feel. It's something you do.
—David Wilkerson

The first bit of restructuring you do comes rather early in a relationship—at the point when you begin to move from the "in-love" state to integrating that love into your whole life.

The issues this brings up will be different in different in different age groups. The younger you are, the simpler your life is, the easier integration is. When you are older and have a more complex life, you will find the process more challenging. However, the older you are and the more experience you have, the easier it is for you to know when and how to restructure.

After you have had some experience with relationships, you have some basic knowledge to use in dealing with the challenges. Once you're a bit older, it is no surprise that the one you love won't change who he or she is in order to become perfectly what you want. This can be a shock when you are younger.

There are, however, many ways to work with the differences.

You should give each other space in which to deal with the parts of your life that you do not share. Work, family responsibilities, hobbies, and old friends all need attention in a well-rounded life. And both of you need time that is not couple time in order to fulfill responsibilities as well as maintain the joy of these tasks.

For the first several weeks or months of a relationship, you may have been inseparable, but this does not mean that you will always be joined at the hip. If each of you does not maintain the things about life that you loved before you met, then sooner or later your relationship will go flat.

You fell in love with this person for who he or she was. If you change that, who will you love?

Jealousy and possessiveness have no place in a good relationship. Certainly each of you will experience moments when you wish the other could give you unlimited time. But the truth is that if you had that kind of focus, you would begin to lament the things you love and no longer have time for.

The farther you get into the relationship, the more you will naturally begin to do things together. Gradually you will begin to have friends who were friends of you both from the beginning. But that must be a gentle and almost automatic thing.

You will also find that it becomes easier to do things together that you both enjoy than to each pursue separate activities all the time. But it is still necessary to have some space in the relationship so that you can have your own growth and your own private time.

As the relationship progresses you will find that there are many times when you need to get to know each other all over again. At the beginning, we tend to make adjustments in a relationship that take it back to the best time, which is usually the beginning. After a few years, though, you have both changed and grown enough that adjusting may mean getting to know each other all over again, exactly as you have become.

Do not mistake this passage for argument. In argument, you are often listening to the other person just enough to defend your point. Instead, take the time to really listen and to let your partner know that you care about what is being said. The only talk you should be doing at this time is to clarify in a gentle way what is being said so that you can really understand it.

There should be no judgment or defensiveness going on as you try to reconnect. This reconnection has to be made between the people the two of you have become, not who you were, so don't bring up old issues that no longer apply just to win your point. The surest way to lose this time is to try to win.

A long-term relationship will go through many changes like this if it is to be successful. When you stop listening and begin to judge, you lose the opportunity to make the necessary adjustments that can take you and your partner happily into your next ten years or so.

To keep the lines of communication open after an adjustment, remember that in a relationship, power games and defensiveness are very destructive. If you use your power to join up and face the world, ready to get involved in the world's business, you are stronger together. But if you use your power against each other to win points, you will lose the relationship that you are trying to control by crushing your partner or forcing him or her to defend themselves against you. It is not worth it.

When you try to gain power or control in a relationship, you are saying that you don't trust your partner. And that is what your partner hears. You also limit their abilities to grow as they need and to celebrate being just exactly who they are. If you love some-one, you need to love them just as they are.

Sometimes It's Not Forever

When one door closes another door opens; but we so often
look so long and so regretfully upon the closed door, that we
do not see the ones which open for us.

—Alexander Graham Bell

First remember that just because the relationship didn't go on doesn't mean your partner wasn't a soul mate. We learn from soul mates. You will understand later that you have learned and grown from this experience; in the meantime, don't let anger and hurt take away the good things that you have experienced.

Beginnings of relationships are a lot of fun; endings seldom are. You need to take some time for readjustment. This readjustment must not be trying to cling to the past. If it is really over, accept it, grieve for it, but don't keep trying to go back, unless that is honestly realistic.

How Do You Know It's Over?

- When he or she has found another partner
- When you have had the breakup discussion and declared it over
- When you have been lying to each other
- When you don't approve of each other's values
- When there has been abuse—physical, verbal, or emotional
- When there is a major addiction to drugs or alcohol
- When control has become the issue
- When the other person stops initiating contact

It is better to know that it is over than to cling to possibilities that have passed. Once you know that it is over you can begin to heal. Healing requires feeling your feelings, and that will not happen if you remain in denial.

Whatever the reasons for the breakup, the relationship has served your growth. It is time to move on now.

Remember that ending a relationship is almost never a joint decision. But it is still a painful experience for both parties. No one wants to have someone leave them. But it is also painful to have to go when you know it will hurt someone who loves and trusts you.

With this change you will have to change your dreams. Because you have experienced this difficult time, however, you will soon construct better dreams.

Surviving a Breakup

First, be sure to cry whenever you need to. This release facilitates healing. It is a chemical process; you will feel better if you let go and do it. And by the way, you *will* stop crying...many people are afraid that if they start crying, they will never stop. But when you have released enough, the tears will end. You will probably sleep and wake the next day feeling a bit better. You will have released a lot of tension.

While you are at it, it is important to feel all of your feelings now. Each little pang is a pang that is dealt with and put away. If you try to ignore them, they will come back when you don't want them and slam you in the back of the head. Just do it now. You'll be better for it.

Don't try to learn the lessons of a relationship while you are still in shock or grief or anger over a breakup. These will come later when you have more perspective. This is a good time to familiarize yourself with the five stages of grief that researcher Elisabeth Kubler-Ross identified; the grief over the end of a relationship is not unlike losing a loved one to death. These are the five stages:

- Denial
- Bargaining
- Anger

- Depression
- Acceptance

Denial

It is easy to get stuck in denial when the breakup process begins. You don't want to change. You have been happy and all you want is to get back to the joy of the better times.

———

Connie called me to get some help getting her relationship "back on track." She told me that she and her boyfriend had been together since high school. They were first loves. They had been attending different colleges for three years, but she said that things had been getting strange for almost a year. When I questioned her closely, she indicated that he had been distancing the relationship. Eventually she admitted that she hadn't seen him for six months. I was beginning to get the picture, but since she seemed to be in touch with him, I suggested that she shouldn't call him for a while. She then admitted to me that "that didn't work." She had already stopped calling him two months before; and he never called her once. Clearly this relationship had ended. She went on to say that he had been seeing someone else for six months, and discussed it with her, and had clearly told her that they were over and she should "get on with her life."

This lady was in some serious denial. She assumed that she still had the relationship and he was just being difficult.

All the time it was clearly over. She and I began working on her accepting it.

———

So you pretend that it is not happening. Sometimes your partner cooperates and denies with you. This stage can last for a while, but you must move through it. That will bring you to the next stage.

Bargaining

"There must be something I can do or say to make him see that I love him," a client said to me yesterday. This was the beginning of her moving out of denial and into bargaining. What she couldn't see, of course, was that whether or not she loved him was not the issue. The issue was that he had moved on and it was no longer vital to him that she loved him.

Sometimes the bargaining happens when you are still maintaining the illusion of a relationship because neither of you really wants to move on, but you both know that it is over. There is a thin line here between a relationship that has really ended and one that can be restored by some restructuring. This exploration may take time, but if the conditions listed under "How Do You Know It's Over?" (see pages 116–17) are present, you are probably just delaying the end.

———

George called me about his girlfriend, "She left me last night, she moved out. She has been planning this for a while," he told me. "But it's okay, because I know that I was wrong and I'll change."

He told me about the relationship. He had known perfectly well that what she needed for it to work, but for over a year he hadn't paid any attention to her when she tried to talk to him about it.

"I know that I was wrong and I was an asshole," he admitted, "but I didn't think she'd do this."

Clearly he had spent the whole relationship taking her for granted and ignoring the things that she tried to communicate to him. Now he was ready to deal.

But his girlfriend had planned this move carefully. A woman will try to make adjustments in a relationship for a long time. But when she has had enough and decides that the guy is never going to listen to her—and that even if he did he would not make the changes she needed—then she reaches the point where it is just over.

She closes down, and her feelings about the man are no longer what they once were. At this point she begins to make changes for her own life, while still technically in the structure of the relationship.

Now her partner is not hearing "complaints," so he thinks that everything is fine. But the truth is that it is already too late. She is gone. She has, of course been gone for some time before he noticed.

George and I talked about this and he seemed to accept it, but he was still sure he could talk her into coming back.

Six months later, she was still gone and he was still thinking she would "come to her senses."

———

Anger

In many ways this a powerful stage of the process. It makes you feel like you are regaining some control as an individual, and that can be quite empowering. It can push you into getting on with your life and when it does that, it is good.

The traps of anger occur when you begin to dwell on the unfairness of it all. If your anger leads you to feeling abused by the situation, it is not at all empowering. In fact, it gives your power away. It also begins a habit of blaming that can only take your personal power farther and farther away.

There is no guarantee of perfect justice in every situation in life. The sooner you learn that, the happier you will be. Expecting justice and lamenting the unfairness of it all is counterproductive in any situation.

Righteous indignation is certainly allowed, but for your own good, it should be in the "I will survive" mode and not the "it's so unfair."

As you begin to see your own power again, remember that this is not power to get even or to show the other person anything, but power to get through it and get on with your life.

Maria was pounding at my door. "Do you have a gun here?" she shouted, "Where can I get a gun tonight, right now?"

Maria had just discovered that her lover of two years was with another woman that night. This was something she had suspected for a long time, but now she knew it for sure. She wanted to find him and shoot him. More precisely, she wanted to use the gun to accomplish roughly what Lorena Bobbit did.

Then she began to sob. For the next hour she alternately sobbed and shouted. She threatened just about everything; her anger was just flying all over the room. I called another friend and we simply just sat there and listened to her and let her go on. Fortunately, no one had a gun. Even if we had, we sure weren't going to turn her loose with it.

After she shouted and talked and cried, eventually we began to laugh about things here and there. Finally we just sat and talked.

It wasn't quite the end of her relationship with that lover, but after that night it was emotionally over. They saw each other a few times and just drifted apart.

Allowing herself to vent all that anger resulted in beginning to accept the end of a relationship that had seldom been good and held very little promise of becoming any better. It was, however, passionate and that was a hard thing to give up.

Sometimes a passionate anger is the best release for a passionate relationship

Depression

This is the "I don't want to try anymore, I'm sick of it, I feel like I've been hit by a truck, I can't deal with anything" stage. Your energy is zapped. You can't work up a good enthusiasm. Even the pain is at a distance; you can't move.

This is part of the healing. Your subconscious has begun to heal you now. The sharp pain of the anger has sapped a lot of energy and its release has left you exhausted. Healing is occurring, but it is taking a lot of energy and you can't find any left for yourself.

There are certain things that will help at this time:

- Allow yourself to experience the sadness. It honors the relationship you have had and the choices you have made.

- Unless this depression last for more than three weeks, don't be tempted to medicate it. This is part of the process of healing and you don't want to get yourself in the habit of using drugs, alcohol, or even herbs to avoid facing your feelings. If you really begin to get concerned after a few weeks, see your doctor or herbalist. It is always better not to medicate if you can avoid it.

- It is important to cry. Tears contain healing chemicals; they are more effective and certainly healthier than any drug you can use. Tears also release some of the emotional pressure.

- When you really feel that you are too depressed to function (which can happen), force yourself to move around. The more exercise you get, the better. Even more natural healing chemicals are released now. Walk, run, ski, play tennis, basketball, do anything that is physical. If there is a bit of anger mixed into your feelings, I recommend tennis. Hitting things can be a very good release, and you get some satisfying exercise. (Don't hit people or animals.)

- Laughing is the final form of healing. We are very lucky to have both television and movies available for this. Everyone has different tastes when it comes to what is appealing at this time; I have personally found the movie *Outrageous Fortune* sufficiently silly and satisfying, especially for a woman. The Thanksgiving episode of *WKRP in Cincinnati* was an absolute cure for me once when I was feeling overwhelmed. And of course, Monty Python can be very effective. I particularly like the flying cow in *The Holy Grail*. The experience of laughing is as releasing as crying is and leaves you in a better mood altogether. Enjoy finding your own laughter medicine.

Remember, this is a period of healing. Allow yourself to heal; believe that you are going to feel better and have a better life soon.

Acceptance

Okay, so you are still not happy about it. But you have begun to find that you can have a life without a partner. You wake up in the morning and you can breathe right away. You begin to think about things besides whether you will see him or her. You begin to think of life as a thing that might be interesting again.

It is not far from here to beginning to take stock of all the new options that life has to offer now that you are on your own. You will think about the people you have found interesting along the way and not pursued because you were in a relationship. You will want to rediscover the sports or activities that your partner did not particularly enjoy.

Possibilities begin to open up. But the best thing is that you feel better. You may still get occasional bursts of anger. You may have a little depression. But overall life is bearable and looking interesting again.

PART FOUR

SOUL RETRIEVAL

I'd rather learn from one bird how to sing
than teach ten thousand stars how not to dance.

—e. e. cummings

After a relationship ends, there needs to be a time when you focus on getting yourself back. During a relationship, you compromise. You give up certain ideas and ways of doing things because the relationship needs it that way. It is not a problem, because the relationship is important to you.

But when the relationship ends, you can choose again. You may be surprised what you choose. You'll probably decide to pick up on things you once enjoyed but let go of during the relationship.

Appropriately, during a relationship you make compromises, not just in the little things you do but in the structure of your life. This is a good idea and it is perfectly healthy to keep a relationship working this way.

But when the relationship ends you need to begin to look at whether or not you still need compromises in your life. They may be just inappropriate; they might be limiting in areas where you no longer need limitations; they might even be things in which you never really believed, but found convenient in working out the relationship.

These issues will not come up all at once. But some might. It may be something as simple as the fact that he didn't like broccoli so you never cooked it, even though you like it. Suddenly you find yourself eating broccoli three times a week and really relishing it.

It may be your idea of what is appropriate to wear or some spiritual beliefs that you have let go of. It can be anything.

This is the time when you get yourself back and discover who you have become without anyone else's opinion of you having any relevance at all. You are precious. Take your time with yourself.

Day by day you will find that your life becomes better and more valuable because it is full of who you really are or, even better, who you have become.

———

Phyllis got a divorce—"finally," according to her friends. She had meant to be married and stay married and she had tried everything to make it work out. But it had ended and she was on her own again.

The first thing she noticed was that the move to her own apartment was easier with only her in charge than it had been with his help. It had taken him forever to hang a picture or a shelf. He would draw diagrams, argue about the height, and never really get it done. She had everything hung up the second day, and by the third she was pretty well settled in.

She had lost her garden and didn't have anyone to cook for. So she began to play tennis. Some new friends came with that game. Her ex wouldn't play tennis with her; he said she was not enough competition, but within a few months, she was winning tournaments.

She discovered that she didn't need to watch sports on TV anymore and began reading. She joined a book club. She met more people.

Sunday mornings she stayed in bed with the newspaper and a croissant.

She had more and more invitations for dates and parties. She was really having a good time. She lost some weight and was radiant. After a few months, she ran into her ex. She told him how many interesting people she had been meeting. He asked her how she had done that. "I learned to just be myself and let everyone see what that was. The people who like me come to talk and the others stay away," she told him.

"Well," he said, "I don't know about that. If I saw you doing that I'd never come near you."

"See," she smiled. "It works."

————

Phyllis could have spent a lot of time lamenting the loss of her husband, her house, and her garden and never explored her real treasure, herself. But she did not do that.

You will find that this time of exploration is one of the most satisfying and productive times of your life. You can do anything. Often the surprise is just learning what you want to do.

This is not the moment to enter into another relationship that will take away from the time you need to find yourself. It is a good moment to meet and get to know many different people and see what suits you as you have become.

Your life right now is not about how you are reflected back in the eyes of another, but how you see yourself. Remember that soul mates provide accelerated growth. If you take the time to feel and act and get to know how you have changed, then your next relationship will bring an even higher level of soul mate into your life.

Obsession Is Not Love

No one can drive us crazy unless we give them the keys.

—Doug Horton

An even more difficult aspect of the end of a relationship happens when you know it is over, it has been over for a while, but your ex keeps coming back—not to stay, just enough to bring your feelings back and make it difficult to forget. Sometimes an ex will go so far as to make it seem like you are going to begin again, only to leave when you seem to be getting close.

You may find her calling just when you have met someone else;

she may turn up where she knows you are going to be. He might begin stopping over to your place, just to be friendly. But it is not friendly if he is playing with your heart.

These people cannot let go but they won't come back either. It begins to make you crazy. You are trying to move on, but just as you rather painfully let go of the old feelings, there your ex is again, rekindling everything.

This is the sort of behavior that begins to kindle obsession. It is actually a kind of mental cruelty. The sanest person can fall into obsession when subjected to this. And the saddest thing is that you will call it love. Obsession is very compelling. It is compelling over the edge of sanity.

It is no wonder we go there. Most of our modern ideas about romance involve either codependence or obsession. There are songs about it. Romance novels try to confuse this with love. It is ingrained in our culture.

Here's how to tell when you are obsessing:

- You can't get the other person out of your mind; no matter what you do, she is all you think about.
- You really don't like him anymore, but you say that you love him.
- You have any suicidal thoughts because of not being with her.
- You do any stalking at all.
- You call and hang up.
- You call even when he is rude to you.
- You drive by her house every chance you get and notice which cars are there and whether the lights are on or not.
- You talk about him and your relationship all the time.
- Your ex is the first thing you think about in the morning and the last thing you think about at night.
- Getting back with her is the only thing you pray for.
- You try to do spells to bring him back. (A really bad idea!)

This obsession seldom happens by itself (unless you have had previous problems with addiction). It is usually the result of back and forth within a relationship that has already broken up. You can neither maintain nor forget the relationship because your ex keeps coming back and holding out the promise of reconnecting (usually sexually) the moment you feel like you can go on alone.

This is a good reason to try to end things very cleanly when they do end, whether you want to or not. It is for your own mental health that you not allow anyone else to pull you into obsession.

Jeff and Sherry had two years of a really nice relationship. They had a lot of fun together and had made plans to make it permanent. Jeff was already acting the role of stepfather to her five-year-old daughter, who adored him.

It was a cozy little domestic scene. Sherry knew that she needed that. She had been a single mother for a few years and had been almost worn out when she met Jeff. He did lots of wonderful little things for her. She might come home from work to a bubble bath and a glass of wine that she could enjoy while he took the baby-sitter home.

Sometimes he would cook a gourmet dinner for her or find a sitter and meet her at a nice restaurant. She really appreciated his thoughtfulness.

When the relationship began, Sherry was the one who was dubious. She didn't really want to get involved just then. She felt her heart had taken a beating from her previous relationship; she thought she should take a break. But every time she opened the door, there was Jeff with a nice surprise. It was very difficult to say no. And she liked him. He made her laugh.

Admittedly, there were times when she really wanted to just stop seeing him and have some time for her. But he was so nice and she had begun to depend on that. He was lovable but she was sure that he loved her more than she loved him. She trusted him.

One weekend when they were at a party at the lake with a

group of friends, he left with another guy to check out another party down the road with more people they both knew. She didn't even think about it.

Then she decided to join a couple of friends to go down to that party. There Jeff was talking to another woman. Sherry got a strange feeling in the pit of her stomach. She went over to him anyway, second-guessing her instincts, and he completely ignored her.

That was it; he was way over the line. She found a ride back to the first party and drove home, angry and shouting at him (he wasn't there) all the way.

He didn't come back to her place that night. He was very distant. He changed their plans the next day so that they wouldn't be alone; he probably felt that she wouldn't make a scene that way. But then he pushed her a little too far and she began to let her anger out at him, and then she drove away.

That should have been the end of it—a little exchange of the stuff they had at each other's places and bye-bye.

She was devastated. She was shocked at how much this had affected her. She also had to try to be strong for her daughter, who was very sad and missed Jeff a lot.

After three weeks of very little contact, she had started to get herself together. She was beginning to go to some social events, and to be able to smile again. And then he called. He asked her to meet him. She went.

This began an off-and-on (but never *too* on) relationship that she was often led to believe was at a new beginning, only to have it fall apart later. The falling apart usually involved the other woman from the party who'd started it all.

Just as she would try to get her life going without him, he found a way to come back. It usually happened when another man showed an interest in her.

She took to driving past his house at odd hours. She also drove past the places where he went socially to see if his car was there. She would call him to see if he was home. (This was before the days of answering machines and caller ID.) She thought about him all the time. She never felt free of him.

One week she knew that he was going to be out of town. She felt like a burden had been lifted. She could go anywhere, certain that she would not see him. She stopped thinking about what he was doing. She began to feel free.

Other things were happening in their lives, too. She got a better job, a job that was more visible in the community. He closed his own business and went to work for a corporation. She was meeting new people all the time, getting invited to all the interesting parties, while his world was growing more restricted. And Jeff had always prided himself in knowing everyone and being included in all of the important community gatherings.

She received an invitation to a rather exclusive opening. He did not. She asked him if he wanted to go as her date. He thought he should have his own invitation. But he agreed to meet her there. He had some plans earlier in the day. She went and waited for him to join her. As she was speaking to some mutual friends and wondering what had become of him, he walked in, hand in hand with his ex-wife.

Sherry was enraged. She excused herself and left the party. Her anger was white hot and then it was gone. The next day she accepted a date. He knew he had gone too far and the phone was silent. She wasn't sad about that; she was, in fact, relieved.

But it wasn't over yet. In fact, even though Sherry thought she had put it behind her and began dating someone else, whom she adored, the moment her new love went out of town on a business trip, there Jeff was again. This time he wanted to really talk, and she knew he was serious.

She met him for a talk and he poured his heart out to her, apologies and all. She didn't give him an answer. On the drive home, she talked to herself: "Here it is, you can have it back now, do you want it?" And she heard the answer from everywhere at once.. *"NO!"*

———

Healing

If only bad habits could be broken as easily as hearts!

—Christopher Spranger

Every person who is single, except for the relatively few who have been widowed, has a string of failed relationships in the past. The older you are, the longer the line gets. If you let your endings get in the way and begin to think of yourself as a failure rather than a learner, you will be building yourself a trap.

If a relationship is not good for you, if it is not quite over but not quite happening, you have to make a decision. It is time to completely put it behind you. You don't want to be stuck hanging on to a relationship that is obviously over.

Because it is over does not mean that this was not a soul mate. Because it is a soul mate is no reason to keep hanging on to a relationship that needs closure. In order to work on a relationship, you need two committed people. If you do not have that, it is time to pack up and move on.

Even if your partner is the one who started the breakup, it will give you a certain power over your life to declare it dead and to act upon that when your ex is still going back and forth.

No matter what reasons were behind the end of your relationship, it was really just the end of a lesson that you learned or taught. Don't try to figure it out right away. If it is going to become clear to you, it will be after all the emotions are put away. Twenty-twenty hindsight needs a little distance.

When you're trying to heal, it is best not to wound yourself any more. Change your schedule so that you won't run into your ex. Once the initial stages of the separation are over, don't spend a lot of time talking about it.

When you speak to mutual friends, talk about other things. They are likely afraid that you will put them in a position of siding with one or the other of you. Don't do it. Even if they try to get you to talk about your ex, just answer briefly and change the subject. Everyone will be more comfortable.

When a couple splits up, friends have a tendency to move away from the individuals involved. The whole dynamic of the friendship has changed, especially if the friends are themselves a couple. Part of this is normal—as your interests and theirs have changed, as have your habits. Don't take it as a personal rejection if these friendships become more distant. Truly, keeping all your mutual friends close will keep you from moving on. And at this time of your life, it is necessary to move on.

If you have been wise, you have kept in touch with the friends you had before the relationship began. Some of these people will have moved on or not be available now, but you can begin to reconnect. Your own friends are the place to begin, and even if you haven't seen them for a long time, you should catch up with them. At this time, give them a brief history of what went on and leave it. Only your best friends and family should be helping you deal with your sadness and frustration. These friends are for the future; don't get them involved in what is now your past.

You want to be operating from strength, and going through every detail of how awful it all was does not very effectively present you as healed and strong. Your private time and perhaps one or two close friends are appropriate for this. But it is not helpful to get stuck in your pain, so try hard not to spend too much time with it. Sometimes a little hard exercise will do a lot more to make you feel better than all the talk in the world.

So begin by clearing the energy around you of the presence of your ex. Move all of the reminders out of your space. Just get a box or two and fill it up...look around to make sure you have every bit of it. There is nothing wrong with getting rid of a little residual anger right now and yelling at your ex while you are doing this. When you have everything gathered up, take the boxes out of your house.

Don't return all of this right away unless your ex has requested it. Stuff it away in the back of the garage, or a storage area, or wherever you won't be running into it anytime soon.

Once this is done, clean your whole house. Stem-to-stern cleaning, with soap and water and furniture oils and vacuuming and maybe even shampooing the upholstery. Don't stop. you can also yell while you do this. The point is to get every skin cell and hair and dust mite that have belonged to the ex out of your home. Stay with this project until the whole place is shiny and clean.

Now go shopping. You want new bedding: sheets, pillowcases, and comforters. You want new colors, maybe even new curtains in the bedroon, towels in the bath. Rearrange the furniture.

Isn't the place starting to feel better? If it is warm enough, open the windows, let fresh air move through the place. If it is cold, just open the curtains up to the sunlight and let it shine.

Now comes the magic part. Go to your local New Age bookstore or metaphysical store or herbal shop or Native American supply store. You want to find some sage smudge sticks. These are little bundles of sweet-smelling sage stems and leaves.

Take these home and burn them like incense (blow out the flame and let it smoke). Now spread this wonderful sweet-spicy-scented smoke all over your house. Pay special attention to the windows and doors, and blow it up into the far corners of rooms, too. Don't forget closets and bathrooms. This smoke will clear all the negative energy…all the remnants not only of your partner's absence, but also of your sadness in dealing with it. That's why I left this ceremony until the end of my discussion about ending a relationship. You do this when all the tears have been shed. When it is time to really forget about it and move on. When you don't want to deal with the ghost of another person in your home anymore.

You can go farther too, and visualize white light around you at a circumference of about three feet out in a globe or egg shape that also goes three feet into the ground. Then visualize the same white light around your house and your neighborhood. This gives you a three-layer density of white light to protect you from negative energy. It will allow unconditional love in but not any emotional residue of less purity.

This is helpful when you believe that your ex may still be sending thoughts or emotions telepathically to keep you attached to the relationship. This may happen if he or she doesn't want to be there anymore, but doesn't completely want to let go either. It keeps you from moving on but doesn't bring back the relationship.

This is a person to whom you were intimately connected. If your connection has not yet been severed, the end of the relationship can bring up frustration and resentment and anger and sadness that find their way through this old, safe passage. It is important to close the door of connection so that these negative emotions don't find their way into your psyche.

Once the doors are closed and your space is cleared, life is a bit easier to live. The future begins as a glimmer of light and then spreads out like a carpet of sunshine. You know that you are ready to move along this brilliant path.

Moving On, Moving Up

Ah, but sooner or later you sleep in your own space.
Either way it's okay, you wake up to yourself.

—Billy Joel

The biggest mistake people make at this point is to try to jump right back into another relationship. Once you are used to doing things two by two, it is uncomfortable to be alone again. But chances are that if you do this, you will jump right back into the same old energy that didn't work in your last relationship.

This is a good time to get your life together, alone, but not lonely. It is time to pick up the things that you put away in favor of a smooth relationship and begin doing the things you have always loved.

Pick up that old guitar. Dust off the piano. Set up the easel and buy fresh paints. Dig into that pile of books you have been meaning to read. Take a walk. Take a run. Buy a dog. Make a garden. Get out your golf clubs. Sharpen your skis. Do the thing you love and arrange your days as you like them. This is a luxury that few moments in our lives give us; indulge yourself.

As you begin to remember the things you like to do, you will begin to recall who you are. You will also get a glimpse at who you are becoming.

If you take some time to process the learning of the past relationship, you will be in a position to meet a soul mate who can take you to a higher level of partnership. It is important to know that the relationship was a valuable experience even if it wasn't forever. Once you understand this and can bless the learning and the time spent with it, then you have opened the door for a much better experience with your next relationship.

If you are still holding anger or resentment or a sense of unfairness, you will not be in a position to meet a person who can carry your relationship experience to a new level.

Relationship is all about learning and growth. You don't get to college until you have completed high school. You don't move on to a higher kind of relationship until you have completed the learning from your previous experience.

Your new knowledge will not have to be relearned, and you will find that you have improved. Once this has happened, the nature of relationship can change and give you a much more satisfying experience.

If you choose this time to increase your knowledge of spiritual matters, you will also increase the potential of finding a more satisfying relationship. This knowledge will change the nature of your goals from the mundane issues of personality to a higher level of awareness in a spiritual partner.

As long as the issues that are important in your life are the same ones you have been working on over and over again, the soul mates whom you attract will be people who are also working on those issues. Once you can get beyond and above the daily issues of habits and power and personality and begin to see yourself working on a higher level of awareness, you will begin to attract a soul mate who is also working there.

Spiritual areas are about unconditional love. People who are comfortable in those areas will be experienced in working on this. Your chances of having a seriously fulfilling relationship improve dramatically if the two of you have this knowledge. Do not expect that you will be able to operate in this unconditional mode with someone you live with. It won't happen; it is too high an expectation. There are conditions to living. There are values and priorities. For instance, if he is still clinging to old power issues, or if she is a bit passive-aggressive, these things are conditions that need to be addressed. Once you have learned unconditional love, it is easier to address these issues lovingly. You are beyond win/lose. You are consciously each other's teacher, and each other's student.

This skill keeps your own life on a higher and more serene level, too, which makes you easier to live with. You will find that you are not so frustrated or easily ruffled. You will be more accepting and generous. Perhaps not every minute, but far more often.

And having a partner who also has this skill brings an additional level of serenity and acceptance into the home. Communication becomes more loving and gentle.

But this is a skill you learn best in those times when you can concentrate on yourself and your own growth. Those times when you are between relationships are the best times to begin.

A strong connection to the spiritual is the best path to finding this ability to love unconditionally. When you allow yourself to have a perspective beyond the day-to-day essentials and to see the big picture, you will find that it is pretty natural.

It is also good to allow unconditional love into your life often and to accept it as love even though it has nothing whatever to do with partnership. Little children, animals, and friends are the best teachers. It is easy to love these creatures unconditionally, because they love you.

A spiritual awareness does not require you to be religious, although that is one path to spiritual awareness. Religions are paths and disciplines that will lead you toward spirituality. Religions have a certain set of beliefs that are designed to get you there. Often, though, you can get trapped in the form of religions and forget the true nature of the quest for connection.

Spirituality is connection to the life force of the universe. It connects us all. It can be called God or Spirit or All That Is. Whatever you choose to name this force, it is personal participation in it that will raise your awareness, gently and easily.

Once you feel this connection, how can you be judgmental? Every soul is a part of your own; every player is intimately connected with you. Everyone contains the light of Spirit as well as the shadow side that gives it its definition and uniqueness.

There are thousands of books and many, many paths toward this knowledge. Choose freely the one that suits you. But be sure that you keep moving along the path toward the light. It is easy to get caught up in the forms and to forget the destination.

Once you have experienced the radiance of this connection, you will find that you can get back there. You will also find that through that radiance, the expression of love can find a whole new meaning.

It is not impossible to find this while you are in a relationship, but it is such a personal experience that it is often easier to achieve in those times when you are alone.

It requires concentration at the beginning. After that it's like riding a bike—it comes right back to you.

Once you have found a personal spiritual connection, you will find that the relationships you attract are at a whole new level of potential.

You may want to rewrite your list of the qualities you want in a partner now, because you know more about what you need and don't need. Once it is time to begin again, begin at the beginning—with deciding what you want.

Begin to feel the presence of the love you are attracting. Now relax and let the universe bring you the person you have been feeling. Don't need, don't hope, don't worry. Your life is important just as it is.

The Wisdom to Know the Difference— Beginning Again With More Clarity

Perhaps the old monks were right when they tried to root love out; perhaps the poets are right when they try to water it. It is a blood-red flower, with the color of sin; but there is always the scent of a god about it.

—Olive Schreiner

Okay. Now it is time to get back on that horse. You have let yourself heal. You have taken the time to get to know who you have become, and you have begun to act upon it.

It is time to honor what you have learned on the whole journey and to take stock again. Go back to the list of your own attributes and change it to reflect your new growth. You need to clearly see your new wisdom and to appreciate its value.

No new relationship will be as important as the relationship you have developed with yourself. It is this knowledge that you now can bring to a richer experience in relationships.

It is time to be open to different kinds of relationships. You needn't look for "the one." Your next soul mate will find you. What you need to do is to spend some time getting to know potential partners. Dating is nice. So few of us do it anymore; we tend to jump right into being a couple almost as soon as we know each other. It's one of the reasons why these relationships come to an end. If we'd taken the time to really get to know each other, we might have made other choices.

When things are working, you will come to know each other slowly and the feelings will only grow as more knowledge unfolds. When things are not right, though, you can avoid a lot of difficulty by recognizing the things that you cannot live with before you get too involved.

The very fact that you have taken the time to get to know yourself again, to get beyond the needy feeling that leads you to accept whatever is offered, will make this experience of relationship more promising.

The truth is that as you have more experiences with relationships, you get better at them. You learn what you need and what you really can't live with. You know what is your problem and what can be assigned to others. You stop feeling any need to play games.

You begin to participate in your own growth, not just expect it to come from another. This sort of growth will attract soul mates of a higher and higher order into your life.

You stop worrying about being "with" someone all the time and begin to look for the quality you want before you decide to jump into a relationship.

You have learned to use your time to develop your own interests instead of waiting for the phone to ring, or wondering whether to call. So you have become a more interesting person. The more interesting you get, the more interesting will be the people who are attracted to you.

The key to all of this, of course, is an increasing consciousness of the experience of your life. You cannot create your life without being conscious of what you are doing. You cannot participate in a high-level soul-mate relationship if you aren't prepared to be absolutely present and conscious in the moments of it.

The moment you go from living on automatic pilot to living in conscious participation, your life changes. It is a bit of work, but the quality of your life will improve so much for it that you will never go back.

Once you learn to be conscious in relationships, you will have the tools to be conscious in all the moments of your life.